WILBERFORCE
— AND —
HULL

Liz Deverell and Gareth Watkins

British Library Cataloguing in Publication Data.
A catalogue record for this book is available from the British Library.

First published 2000

© 2000 Liz Deverell and Gareth Watkins
All photographs © respective owners as indicated

Published by Kingston Press

All rights reserved. No part of this publication may be reproduced, stored in a retrieval system, or transmitted, in any form, or by any means, electronic, mechanical, photocopying, recording, or otherwise, without prior written permission of the publishers.

This book is sold subject to the condition that it shall not, by way of trade or otherwise, be lent, resold, hired or otherwise circulated, in any form of binding or cover other than that in which it is published, without the publisher's prior consent.

The Authors assert their moral right to be identified as the Authors of the work in accordance with the Copyright Design and Patents Act 1988.

ISBN 1 902039 07 6

Kingston Press is the publishing imprint of Kingston upon Hull City Libraries,
Central Library, Albion Street, Kingston upon Hull, England HU1 3TF
www.hullcc.gov.uk/kingstonpress

Printed by Kingston upon Hull City Council Printing Services,
1-5 Witham, Kingston upon Hull, England HU9 1DA

Authors' preface

This short life of William Wilberforce does not claim to be a work of original research. Excellent scholarly biographies of Wilberforce already exist and have provided the basis for this book. Our intention here is to place a little more emphasis on Wilberforce's early years and to give a rounded and lively picture of Hull, his birthplace and the town where he grew up. Wilberforce achieved lasting national and international fame for his great contribution to the abolition of slavery but the people of Hull will never forget that his roots were here.

Liz Deverell, Gareth Watkins
July 2000

Acknowledgments

Authors' Acknowledgements
Liz Deverell and Gareth Watkins would like to offer their sincere thanks to all those who have helped with the production of this book.
We are grateful to our friends and colleagues at Hull Central Library: Steve Howard from Kingston Press for his constant patience and gentle encouragement, Paul Winn, Jan Shaw, Joanne Wilkinson, and members of staff in the Local Studies and Arts and Humanities Libraries whose advice and support did much to facilitate the writing of the text.
We have received much assistance from staff in other departments of Hull City Council: Ann Bukantas, Arthur Credland and Phil Burton (Museums and Galleries), Geoff Oxley and his staff at the City Archives, Geoff Sharpe (Graphic Design), Liz Hampton (Modern Records), Andrew Walmsley (Printing) and Peter Lawson (Corporate Marketing). We are particularly grateful to the staff - both curators and attendants - at Wilberforce House for their ready co-operation in this project and would especially like to thank Clare Parsons, Assistant Keeper of Social History, for her assistance and advice; her contributions have done much to improve the book and are much appreciated.
Chris Ketchell kindly gave us guidance on a number of points, and Andre Brannan scanned diligently through local newspapers of the period and unearthed a number of hitherto obscure references to Wilberforce: we thank them both.
Many other individuals helped with information, illustrations, advice or encouragement: Judith Preston Anderson, Anthony David Baynes, Melanie Blake, Alex Clarke, John Croft, Pat Doyle, Jean Fenwick, Jude Fox, Sally George, James Kilvington, Suzy Luck, Ian Mason (East Riding County Archivist), John McSherrie MBE, Geraldine Mulcahy, Barbara Robinson, Jenny Stanley, Mr James and Mrs Jean Wrangham. We would particularly like to thank Lord Richard Wilberforce for his kindness and his co-operation in this project.
We are particularly indebted to Dr. David Neave, who read through an early draft of the first six chapters and made a number of suggestions and corrections: all those errors which remain are, of course, the responsibility of the authors.

Publisher's Acknowledgements
Kingston Press would like to thank Lord Richard Wilberforce for providing the foreword to the book, Councillor Patrick Doyle for writing the introduction, Liz Deverell for writing the text of chapters 1 - 6 and Gareth Watkins for the text of chapter 7 and the picture research.

Contents

Foreword	page i
Introduction	page ii
Chapter 1: The time and place	page 1
Chapter 2: Family and early childhood	page 7
Chapter 3: Later childhood and youth	page 18
Chapter 4: Early manhood and first seven years as MP	page 30
Chapter 5: Wilberforce and slavery	page 39
Chapter 6: The elder statesman	page 56
Chapter 7: Hull and its most famous son	page 68
Notes	page 82
Works consulted	page 84
List of photographs and illustrations	page 87
Index	page 91

Foreword
by Lord Wilberforce

Shakespeare and Stratford, Wordsworth and Grasmere, the Brontes and Haworth: history abounds with associations of individuals of distinction and their families with places where they were brought up and from which they drew their strength. None is more real than that between William Wilberforce and Hull; that is well enough known. All his biographies have emphasised and explored it; all, to some extent have seen the relevance of his family's history as firmly rooted in East Yorkshire and for several generations in Hull.

This attractive and well researched publication presents the association as bilateral, placing the development of Hull from a medium sized walled city into a modern, expanding international port side by side with the contribution of one of its citizens and his family culminating in his election as Member of Parliament for Hull in 1780. The authors have be able to draw on material in the City and County archives, in local histories, in the Brynmor Jones Library, on the one side, and in family papers, correspondence and diaries, interacting upon each other so as to give a picture of a family rooted in and drawing strength from the City, and of a City able to take pride in the family's presence.

By William's death in 1833 his sons had moved south, leaving Wilberforce House to the market, and his descendants' careers have been widely spread over England but the association remained real and alive. Much was done in the years when William's statue was beginning to receive renewed recognition, notably by his great-granddaughter Mrs Arnold Reckitt of Brantinghamthorpe who took a special interest in the restoration of Wilberforce House and the relocation of William's column. I was myself greatly privileged to have taken part in the centenary celebrations of 1933 so splendidly organised by the City Corporation, and in the reopening of Wilberforce House in 1983 and it was a great source of pride when I was able to take my title from the City of Kingston upon Hull.

This book makes the period of William Wilberforce's life (1759-1833) in an important corner of England come alive and gives new and stimulating insights into the local and national condition which made possible the engagement and lifelong devotion of William Wilberforce to the abolition of the slave trade and to ultimate emancipation.

Introduction
by the leader of Kingston upon Hull City Council, Councillor Patrick J. Doyle

William Wilberforce's monument dominates Queens Gardens, and the people of Kingston upon Hull should be enormously proud of their most famous son. Wilberforce was born in the family home on High Street (now a museum and memorial to his anti-slavery campaign). He was baptised in the font, which still stands in Holy Trinity, and first educated in the Grammar School, which lay in the shadow of the Church. Later Hull became his first parliamentary constituency. That pilgrims' trail from High Street, to Holy Trinity, to the Old Grammar School, and the Monument is one taken by many Africans, Afro- Caribbeans and Afro-Americans paying tribute to their Emancipator. Our twin city of Freetown, Sierra Leone was established as a settlement for free slaves by Wilberforce's supporters and significantly one village is called Wilberforce. Wilberforce's legacy continues to this day, with the Anti-Slavery Association having on its committee Members of Parliament for Hull, and campaigns continue to abolish debt bondage, child labour, child prostitution, etc.

The City decided a few years ago to honour Wilberforce's memory by instituting an annual lecture, at which the speaker (chosen for their contribution to the case of civil liberties), shall be given the Wilberforce Medallion, inscribed with the original campaign's slogan "Am I not a man, a brother?" Last year Her Majesty the Queen bestowed the medal on Archbishop Desmond Tutu, who later that day gave a memorable address on indebtedness, Jubilee 2000 and the message of Wilberforce. Each year the Emancipator's death and achievements are commemorated in a simple service, originally at Wilberforce House and now at the Monument.

We hope that this book highlighting the links between this great man and the city port of Hull will be read widely, and that our citizens, in the spirit of Wilberforce, will always champion the cause of liberty, of civil rights and humanity.

Chapter 1

The time and place

Medieval Hull received its first town charter from Edward I in 1299. In the seven hundred years since then Hull has changed and grown out of all recognition; but in 1759, the year in which William Wilberforce was born, most of the changes were yet to come and Hull was still essentially a medieval walled port. What was it really like to live there, to grow up in Hull in the middle part of the eighteenth century? In order to bring Wilberforce to life we need to take a close look at the town where he was born, and, briefly, at the wider picture of Britain at that time.

In 1759 George II had been on the throne for thirty-two years and was about to be succeeded - in 1760 - by his grandson George III. Britain was entering a period of increasing wealth, stability, power and influence. British and French forces were still fighting each other for colonial supremacy in places around the globe (and would do so for another half-century). But by the end of the Seven Years War in 1763, Britain had the basis of its Empire: colonies along the East coast of North America, including parts of what is now Canada; trading posts in Bombay and Calcutta; and islands in the West Indies, where enslaved Africans had been working the sugar plantations on the Spanish-owned islands for the previous two centuries.

With all these markets for British exports, intercontinental trade - including, of course, the slave trade - flourished. The British merchant fleet trebled in size between 1695 and 1760, and ports like Bristol, Liverpool and, for a short time, Whitehaven, on the west coast of Britain, expanded to service the trade routes across the Atlantic.

Hull, on the east coast, was on the 'wrong' side of the country for the burgeoning transatlantic trade, but its position was ideal for the already well-established trade routes to Scandinavia and to German and Dutch ports, especially Amsterdam. By the 1750s, Russia was commercially developed enough to to be exporting timber and iron: the port of Hull was taking a large proportion of these goods and Hull merchants had close links with the Baltic ports of Riga, Narva and St. Petersburg.

Hull in the 1750s was a prosperous port, but still small compared to some others around the English coast. The 'port' consisted of a three-quarter mile stretch of the River Hull - called the Haven or sometimes the Old Harbour - extending from the Humber up to North Bridge where the town walls met the river. The west bank was lined with the warehouses, business premises and living quarters of the wealthy merchants whose rather grand houses fronted onto High Street.

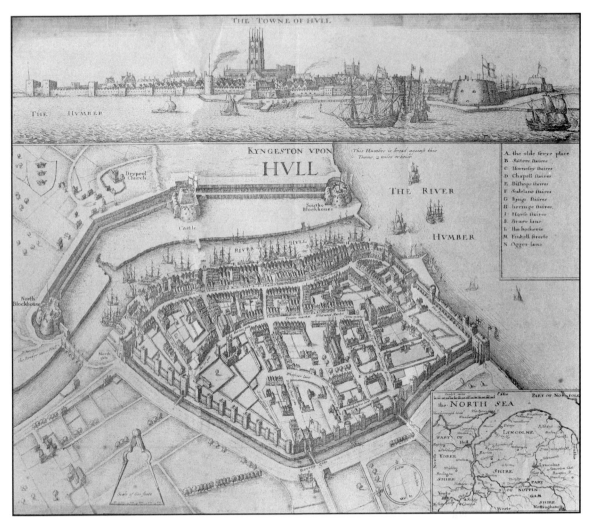

1. (Below) Bird's eye view of "Kyngeston upon Hull" in 1640 by Wenceslaus Hollar, showing the town just before the outbreak of the Civil War. (Above) South-east view of Hull from the Humber.

By the time Wilberforce was born in 1759 (in the house which was later numbered 25 High Street), the Haven was notoriously congested: ships often collided with each other, and the narrowness of the waterway caused long delays. The need for improved docking facilities was a great subject of debate within the town and eventually led to the opening of the country's first enclosed dock, later known as Queen's Dock, in 1778.

The town of Hull was still essentially medieval in appearance. Approaching either by land or from the sea, the visitor would see fortifications. On the north and west sides were ditches and then the brick walls, towers and occasional gates of the old defences. The wall continued round the south side facing the Humber and on the east, across the waters of the Haven, was the more modern Garrison - often called the Citadel - which in about 1690 replaced, or rather incorporated, the castle and one of the blockhouses that Henry VIII had had constructed to protect the town on its exposed eastern flank. Up to the 1760s, town laborours were still working on the upkeep of the city walls and the ditches, drawbridges and gates along the walls, although it might have been a losing battle - John Wesley, visiting Hull to preach in 1752, was surprised at the "miserable conditions of the fortifications ... ruinous and decayed".[1]

While the walls lasted they marked the boundaries of the town. Outside the walls was a flat land of watery fields, with often boggy tracks radiating out from the town, although the turnpiking[2] of the three major roads from Hull - to Kirkella, Beverley and Hedon - in the 1740s had made local travel by cart or carriage much easier. Inside the walls

2. Beverley Gate, Hull. Drawn by Benjamin Gale in 1776, shortly before it was demolished.

was crammed a population of possibly 12,000 people, 3000 *more* than when Daniel Defoe, in 1726, described Hull as "exceedingly close built ... extra-ordinary populous, even to inconvenience, no room to extend it self by buildings".[3] A plan of 1640 by Wenceslaus Hollar shows the medieval network of streets - streets that we still walk today - with long gardens behind the houses: but a century later there was much piecemeal building over these spaces to accommodate the growing population. Many of the original timber-framed houses which had lined the narrow streets had either been knocked down and replaced in brick, or sometimes were being built higher, new storeys added as and when necessary. Behind the street fronts, labourers and artisans had to crowd with their families into congested courts. Paupers, orphans, the old and the sick who did not possess even a roof over their heads might end up in the workhouse, Charity Hall, on Whitefriargate near the city walls, although, if they were well-behaved, the aged poor would have the chance of accommodation in one of the town's many almshouses.

3. Plan of Hull c.1770, by Thomas Jeffreys. The town is still contained within its medieval walls; the main development since the time of Hollar's plan (Fig. 1, above) has been the construction of the massive Garrison on the eastern, Drypool, side of the River Hull.

The lives of the poor must have been hard and often wretched. There was no medical attention unless a doctor could be afforded. There was no education for their children except for two free schools, one for boys and the small Charity School for twenty poor girls, founded by Alderman William Cogan, where they were taught how to be household servants. Punishment for small crimes was often transportation. Men could be press-ganged into the Navy. The entertainments of the poor were cock-pits, billiard halls and the comfort to be found in the many public houses and dram shops. However, the poor of Hull had one great advantage over their contemporaries in other towns: and this was the benign rule of the merchants.

From the seventeenth century onwards the local government of Hull had been in the hands of a small elite group of merchants grown prosperous on the Baltic and North Sea trade, and who were, in the main, public-spirited and conscientious. In the eighteenth century gracious merchant houses were still being built right among the tenements and mean cottages on the crowded medieval streets. The rich were thus unable to ignore the poor, and the town improvements introduced by the Aldermen of Hull during the eighteenth century benefitted rich and poor alike. Streets and alleys were paved, rudimentary street lighting was introduced and scavengers were appointed to clear the streets. Collection points were organised outside the city walls for human and animal waste which was needed as manure by East Riding farmers. New sewers were laid; and Alderman Wilberforce, William's grandfather, was financially involved in the erection of waterworks for the supply of fresh water, and the laying of pipes in the streets. In 1755 the Corporation even introduced parking regulations, prohibiting carts, waggons and carriages from standing in the narrow streets longer than was needed to unload goods or people.

The names of the greatest of these merchant families of the eighteenth century are still familiar today as the names of families, houses, buildings, businesses and streets in modern Hull and East Yorkshire - Thornton, Blaydes, Maister, Pease, Broadley, Sykes, Crowle, Mowld - and, of course, Wilberforce.

4. The East Riding of Yorkshire in 1610, showing the locations of Wilberfoss, Pocklington, Beverley and Hull.

Chapter 2

Family and early childhood

There is a small village eight miles east of York called Wilberfoss. Here, for many generations after the Norman Conquest, lived the predecessors of the Wilberforce family. In the sixteenth century a younger son moved to Beverley, and this branch of the family flourished. In 1642 William Wilberforce's great-great-great-grandfather was mayor of Beverley at the time of the Civil War. Later generations were prosperous and well-respected tradesmen - mercers and woollen drapers - with a tradition of public service as aldermen. The family name remained Wilberfoss until the beginning of the eighteenth century.

William's grandfather, born in 1690, was a prominent figure in Hull by the time William was born. He moved to Hull from Beverley as a youth to be apprenticed to the merchant John Thornton in his counting house in High Street and in due course married Thornton's daughter, Sarah, in 1711. William's grandfather was obviously merchant material. He also had money, having inherited valuable property from his mother and he quickly joined the group of Hull merchants drawing their profits from the Baltic trade. He was soon elected as an alderman (a public office held for life), and was twice mayor of Hull, once in 1722, when he was only thirty-two, and again in 1740.

5. Hull Sugar House, the huge sugar refinery in Lime Street, 1735. Built by Godfrey and William Thornton, probably in conjunction with their brother-in-law Alderman William Wilberforce.

Alderman William and his wife Sarah Wilberforce made their home at number 25 High Street, which became their property on the death of John Thornton in 1732. Their son, Robert, born in 1728, was the youngest of eleven children, most of whom were baptised at the nearby parish church of St. Mary, in Lowgate. His older brother, William, (the only other boy to survive infancy), moved away to London and Robert became a partner in his father's business. He got married young - to Elizabeth Bird, sister of Alderman

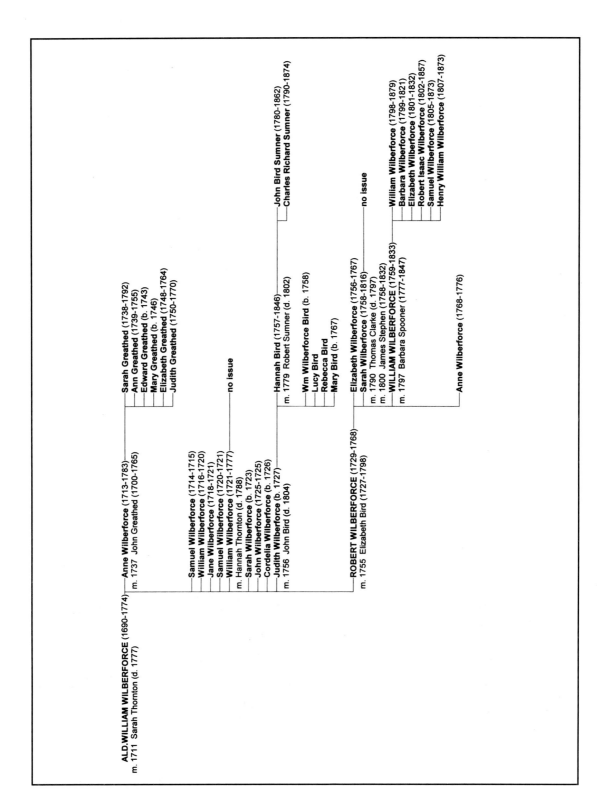

6. *Descendants of Alderman William Wilberforce of Hull.*

7. St Mary's Lowgate, Hull, c.1796.

John Bird of London - and they produced four children. William, the future MP, was the only boy, and of his three sisters only one, Sarah (known always as Sally), survived to adulthood.

Alderman Wilberforce retired to North Ferriby in 1755, leaving the running of the family firm to Robert. So by the time William was born, in August 1759, the family living 'over the shop' in the house in High Street consisted of Robert and Elizabeth with their eldest child, Elizabeth, aged three, and eighteen-month-old Sally. This little family would, of course, have been augmented by servants, including a nursemaid for the children.

The family home

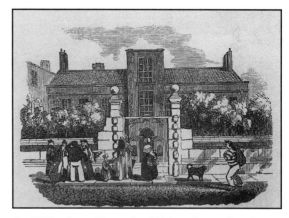

8. Wilberforce House in 1835 – the earliest known view of the building.

What was the house like in the early 1760s? Luckily the building itself still stands, and the frontage, set back behind a seventeenth century wall is just as it was at that time. The house was built in the 1660s by Hugh Lister, reputedly on the site of a house where Charles I was entertained by Sir John Lister in 1639. The Wilberforces acquired the house in 1732 and made extensive alterations. The outside remained much the same except that the brick mullioned windows were replaced by bigger sash windows, giving more light to the rooms. A new grand staircase was installed in about 1760, because the big double house next door to the north, built in the 1750s, was taking light from the old staircase and from the counting house window. (This handsome building, still standing, is known now as 'the Georgian Houses' and is part of Hull Museums).

9. *Wilberforce House, the staircase and Venetian window, surmounted by vine trail plasterwork around a Wilberforce eagle crest.*

10. *Wilberforce House, view of the stairwell ceiling showing the Wilberforce eagle*

11. The "Georgian Houses", 23-24 High Street. Built for the Wilberforce's next-door neighbour James Hamilton, Baltic merchant, shortly after 1756. Photograph by Bill Marsden 1997.

12. Wilberforce House, the nursery in 1884. Tradition has it that Wilberforce was born in this room.

The inside of Wilberforce House, as it came to be called, has been much remodelled since the 1750s. It became a bank; and then, in the nineteenth century, it passed out of the family and the rooms were subdivided into offices for various different businesses. It is therefore difficult now to wander round the rooms as they are and feel close to the family who lived there two hundred and fifty years ago. But although the inside has been so changed, there is enough historical and architectural evidence for us to be able to take a broader view and imagine what a visitor might see and hear when she paid a call on the Wilberforce family in the the summer of 1760.

The visitor - perhaps a lady of one of the other great merchant families - would approach up the narrow paved High Street, passing on her left the grand new house (now number 160) built for the Maister family. Another fifty yards would bring her to the Wilberforce residence, and she would turn right through the imposing gateway, perhaps casting a glance upwards at the window of the small first-floor room which is reputed to have been the nursery. As the visitor was welcomed in she would admire the newly erected staircase with its fashionable carved balusters; and she would be aware on her left of the busy counting house - the room where all the records, ledgers and account books of the family firm were kept in order.

If the visitor ventured out into the busy area at the back of the house she would be familiar with all the activity taking place in the space between the house and the River Hull, although a visitor now will see only a quiet garden, and a river empty apart from an occasional barge. At that time this space was filled with all the equipment needed to service the private staith, where the sailing ships crowded in to unload their cargoes: timber from Norway for the Hull shipyards: iron from Sweden for the Sheffield steelworks; and hemp and flax from Russia for the manufacture of rope and canvas, and for the Lancashire linen industry. We can get some idea of how much else, apart from the house itself, was crammed into this narrow piece of land from the will of Robert Wilberforce, written in 1764:

" ... my house in the High Street in Kingston upon Hull wherein I dwell with all the Outhouses Warehouses Cellars Staiths Staith Chambers Granaries Scales Scale Beams Scale Weights Gardens Pumps Pipes of Wood or Lead and other appurtenances thereto ... "[4]

This house, and this busy, bustling, noisy workplace just behind, was where William spent the first formative years of his life.

Early childhood

William Wilberforce was born on 24 August 1759 and baptised one month later at Holy Trinity church. Unfortunately, little is recorded of William's early years apart from a few anecdotes in the *Life of William Wilberforce*, a biography produced by two of William's sons after his death. We are told that William was a delicate little boy, small for his age and rather puny, with the bad eyesight from which his mother also suffered. But he was bright, intelligent, affectionate and apparently unusually considerate for a small boy. "I shall never forget, says a frequent guest at his mother's, how he would steal into my sick room, taking off his shoes lest he should disturb me, and with an anxious face looking through my curtains [i.e. round the four-poster bed] to learn if I was better."[5] One could, of course, interpret this little story as an example of childish curiosity, rather than solicitude for the well-being of the guest.

Apart from these few facts, we have to imag-

13. The font at Hull Holy Trinity Church.

ine the sort of life he experienced as a small boy. He would certainly have found continual excitement in what was happening just behind the house. He must often have been taken down to the staith to watch the big ships - (big to a young boy, although they would seem very small to us now) - manoeu-

12

14. Aston Hall North Ferriby, residence of Alderman William Wilberforce until his death in 1774. Drawing by Suzy Luck, 1982.

vering to land, foreign sailors shouting to each other as they lowered the flapping sails. Once the ships were unloaded, William would have watched the goods being manhandled onto horse-drawn sledges for transport to the various warehouses. Perhaps sometimes on wet days his father took him into the counting house to meet the clerks busy with their ledgers. The merchant families of Hull had a busy social life, especially as so many of them were inter-related; so William would often have accompanied his mother on visits to other families, and played with, for example, the young Sykeses and Thorntons, forming friendships which lasted into adulthood.

Going a little further afield, William also had trips to North Ferriby, seven miles from Hull along the Humber, to visit his grandfather. Alderman Wilberforce had retired to a rather grand mansion, later known as Aston Hall, on High Street, North Ferriby (now demolished). The journey there by carriage would have been quite an adventure for a small boy: the road to North Ferriby was not turnpiked until the next century so it would have been a bumpy ride.

The Grammar School

When William was seven years old he was enrolled at the Grammar School, "going daily from his father's house to school with his satchel on his shoulder." He would already have known many of his fellow-pupils - sons of the merchants, the shipowners and the more prosperous tradesmen.

15. Hull Grammar School in 1835 - the earliest known illustration.

The Grammar School that William attended was built at the end of the sixteenth century, replacing an earlier grammar school endowed by Bishop Alcock in 1479. After 1548 Hull Corporation took over financial responsibility for the running of the school and it was the Corporation that, in 1583, put up the two storey building we see today (now a museum) on South Church Side, facing on to the open square dominated by Holy Trinity church. Some of the cost of construction was probably met by the Hull Merchants Company, as the upper floor was added to the building for them to use as a hall. By the time William started there in 1766 the building was already nearly two hundred years old, although it had been refurbished in the 1660s when the interior columns were placed down the centre of the schoolroom. A small fireplace, still to be seen, had been installed in 1734. At the time William was at the school the upper storey was occupied by a little private school unconnected with the more prestigious Grammar School below.

Soon after William joined the school its most famous master, Joseph Milner, a brilliant scholar and Cambridge graduate, was appointed under the auspices of Alderman Wilberforce, and Milner installed his seventeen-year-old brother, Isaac, as usher to help with the teaching of the younger boys. The Milner brothers came from a poor weaver's family in Leeds. Isaac, hungry for knowledge but from a family too poor to finance a second son's education, had spent the previous five years at a loom with Latin texts propped in front of him. Isaac went on to be a nationally renowned academic and churchman: he became a lifelong friend to Wilberforce, and had a profound effect on his moral development (see Chapter 4). The one anecdote we have of William at this time, quoted in the sons' biography, is from Isaac:

> "Even then his elocution was so remarkable ... that we used to set him upon a table and make him read aloud as an example to the younger boys."

The education delivered to the merchants' sons was the typical 'gentlemen's' classical education of the time, based mainly on the grammar and the translation of Latin and Greek texts. However it seems that Isaac contributed lessons in algebra; and some history, geography and study of the English language was introduced about this time. Joseph Milner was thus a progressive schoolmaster, and he was also remembered as a kind man, using the cane very sparingly. The boys were obliged to attend services at Holy Trinity on Sundays: this would have made William familiar with both the great churches in Hull, for his family home was in the parish of St. Mary Lowgate, his grandfather having been several times churchwarden there.

William's daily journey as he walked to and from school must have been a education in itself. On leaving the house he would immediately have been confronted with powerful and unpleasant smells - from the oil seed mills, the tar yards and the whale-blubber refiners. His route to school would have brought him, via the very narrow, cobbled Chapel Lane or Bishop Lane, into the busy Market Place where he would have seen in the distance the equestrian statue of King William III (still there, and known familiarly as King Billy), and beyond, the gaol and the guildhall. Before reaching the statue he would have turned right along South Church Side beside the towering Holy Trinity Church to join his fellow students at the grammar school.

Any visitor to Hull now can follow this route; but it needs imagination to people these streets as they were in the 1760s. Forget the Victorian banks and the twentieth century office blocks. Imagine instead streets lined with a mixture of tumbledown houses and gracious terraces, and crowded with carts and carriages: public houses disgorging drunken mariners: ladies and gentlemen exchanging social pleasantries with each other: children playing in the gutter: little shops and businesses spilling onto the street; and in between, glimpses through tunnel entrances into the cramped slums behind. This is what William would have seen every day. It would not be surprising if his later efforts to improve the lives of the poor were to some extent the result of his childhood experience in Hull.

16. 179 High Street Hull; the house opposite the Wilberforce's residence. From a drawing by F.S.Smith dated 1887. Shows the timber-framed jettied construction typical of many of the older buildings in High Street at the time Wilberforce was born.

17. 1796 view of "King Billy", the equestrian statue by the Flemish sculptor Peter Scheemakers which was erected in 1733. The statue now stands over a set of gentlemen's conveniences, built 1901-2.

18. The old Hull Guildhall and Prison, which formerly stood at the south end of the Market Place, c.1780.

19. Hull Holy Trinity Church 1796. This view shows the Market House which formerly stood at the eastern end of the church and was demolished shortly after the date of this drawing.

20. William Wilberforce in his twelfth year (1770), after John Russell. Presumably painted whilst he was living with his uncle and aunt in Wimbledon. By kind permission of the trustees of the late C.E.Wrangham.

Chapter 3

Later childhood and youth

Very little is recorded about William's eldest sister Elizabeth, except for her baptism at Holy Trinity Church in August 1756. When reminiscing late in life to his sons he recalled that she had died while at boarding school in London, when he was about eight years old. At that time, for a girl to be educated at all outside the home was unusual, and private boarding schools for girls were only just beginning to appear. It is difficult to imagine why she should have been sent away to school, especially since the boys of William's generation and background were educated locally, at Hull, Beverley and Pocklington Grammar Schools. Whatever the cause, Elizabeth's death must have brought grief to the family, especially as it happened probably in the same year as the death of the head of the household. Robert, the young father of four children, died in the family house in March 1768, aged thirty-nine. His youngest daughter, Ann, who survived him by only eight years, had been born just months before his death.

21. St Mary's church, Beverley, in 1829.

Robert directed in his will that he should be buried "with the least shew of funeral pomp" at St. Mary's Church in Beverley, near to the resting place of his mother and grandmother Wilberforce. We may imagine the sad funeral procession, perhaps led by his young widow and his father the Alderman, on its journey from the house in High Street out through the old town walls and then northwards for seven miles along the newly turnpiked road through Woodmansey to Beverley.

Following the death of Robert, the Wilberforce family business was restructured. Alderman Wilberforce had astutely built links with the wealthy Smith family of Nottingham, founders of the country's first provincial bank and had taken on Abel Smith II as an apprentice in 1732. The Smiths no doubt saw the advantages of adding some commercial skills to their banking operations. The family links were further cemented by marriage, for Abel Smith had become Robert's brother-in-law by marrying Mary Bird, Robert's wife's sister. Abel Smith was by now a middle-aged man, very much part of Hull society and thoroughly experienced in the financial affairs of the family business. So it was in the natural way of things that, when Robert Wilberforce died, he should take control. He put his son, Abel Smith III (William's cousin), in charge of the business; it then became 'Wilberforce and Smith'.

Mrs Wilberforce decided - or it was decided for her by Alderman Wilberforce, the head of the family - that William should be put in the care of his uncle William, Robert's elder brother, who had married his first cousin, Hannah Thornton and moved to London to work with the London branch of the Thornton family, in his father-in-law's firm. By the time William came to stay in 1769, William and Hannah had been married for many years but had no children themselves. William became as dear to them as a son.

Life in London

William soon settled in with his aunt and uncle. Their town house was in St. James's Place, in London's West End, close both to the formal gardens of St. James's Park and to the Mall where the fashionable people promenaded. The Wilberforces also had a villa in Wimbledon (then, of course, out in the countryside). But William did not have very much time to enjoy either residence because his aunt and uncle enrolled him in a second-rate little boarding school in Putney, just south of the river. In later life Wilberforce told his son that he had been taught a bit of

22. Abel Smith II (died 1788), the uncle of William Wilberforce.

23. *William Wilberforce and Hannah Thornton, portrait by Joseph Highmore; presumed to have been painted at the time of their wedding c.1750. William's uncle and aunt, with whom he lived from 1769 to 1771.*

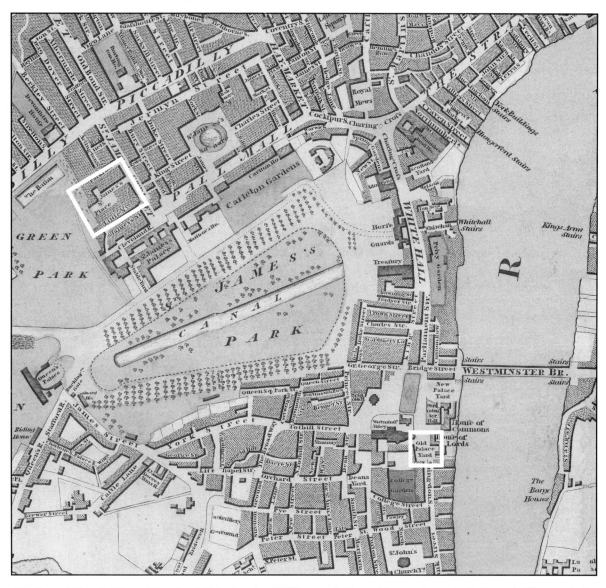

24. Part of Mogg's Plan of London 1810, showing William and Hannah's town house in St James's Place and also Old Palace Yard, where William Wilberforce lived when he was an MP.

25. *John Wesley.*

everything - writing, French, arithmetic, Latin - but nothing in depth. He did not like the Scottish usher, red-bearded, who only shaved once a month; and he hated the food:

"I was sent at first among the lodgers and I can remember even now the nauseous food with which we were supplied, and which I could not eat without sickness."

William's aunt and uncle were devout Methodists. At that time Methodism was a religious movement within the Church of England: John Wesley, an Anglican clergyman, started it in 1738 after he experienced an intense feeling of personal salvation by God. Wesley began to travel all over the

26. *George Whitfield Preaching.*

country, attracting huge crowds to his meetings - often held in the open air. Over the years he is thought to have visited Hull on fifteen occasions. Wesley's message had enormous appeal for the masses of the population; but more influential among the upper classes was George Whitfield, the great Evangelical preacher, who travelled in America as well as England. These two men and their followers preached a message of salvation in which the most important elements were a personal experience of conversion, close attention to the words of the Christian gospels, and a duty to bring others into the fold. William's aunt and uncle admired George Whitfield and counted him as a personal friend. Although it is unlikely that their nephew actually met him or heard him preach, William would have mixed frequently with other dedicated Methodists when he was not at school. His aunt would almost certainly have taken him to Clapham to the house of her half-brother, John Thornton, who had been converted by George Whitfield fifteen years before. In fact there is an anecdote in William's sons' biography to the effect that John Thornton once gave him an unusually large sum of pocket money - with the proviso that some of it should be given to the poor.

The religious fervour of William and Hannah Wilberforce had a great effect on their nephew. After two years with them he was, he remarked in later life, "completely a methodist". His interest in religion began to worry his mother. Like most Anglicans she had a deep dislike of any form of Evangelicalism. Alderman Wilberforce shared his daughter-in-law's concern:

"if Billy turns Methodist he shall not have a sixpence of mine".

Mrs Wilberforce hurried down to London to fetch her son home. His aunt begged his mother not to take him away from the opportunity of a religious life; his mother gave a contemptuous reply; and back he came to Hull in 1771 at the age of twelve.

School at Pocklington

William was broken-hearted, for his aunt and uncle had loved him as if he were their own son and he had returned that love. However his family and friends in Hull were determined to wean him as soon as possible from what they saw as the harmful effects of his stay with the Methodists. The first problem was where to send him to finish his schooling. The Grammar School was now out of the question because Joseph Milner, the schoolmaster, had been converted to religious 'enthusiasm' during William's absence in London. His reputation collapsed and he was despised and ridiculed for his energetic efforts to save sinners, both in and out of the pulpit. It was decided to send William as a boarder to Pocklington Grammar School, twenty miles away just off the road to York (and only five miles from the village of Wilberfoss where his family originated).

It was not unusual for the sons of Hull's merchant class to attend the Pocklington school, especially in periods when Hull Grammar School's reputation dipped. In 1771, however, Pocklington School was also going through a low patch - there were only about thirty pupils, compared to well over a hundred a century before. The headmaster, the Reverend Kingsman Baskett, was apparently a man of the world rather than an academic and the pupils were not forced to work. Mr. Baskett was paid a high fee for William's schooling and it is likely that William was specially treated. Whereas other boarders were lodged with families in the village, William had a room in the Master's house and may well have dined with him and had individual tuition. Wilberforce himself looked back on his five years at Pocklington as passed in idleness, although he acquired a good knowledge of the classics and English poetry. He was probably a weekly boarder: he certainly spent many weekends in a round of visits to the local gentry.

This new life of idleness and pleasure must have seemed very alien to William at first, torn so recently from the devout and loving uncle and aunt in London. For years afterwards he wrote sad and secret letters to them both which demonstrate clearly and pathetically how much he missed them and how hard he tried to cling on to his religious faith.

It was home life, rather more than the school environment, which was eventually to wipe out the young boy's preoccupation with religion. Wilberforce remembered that:

"the religious impressions which I had gained at Wimbledon continued for a considerable time after my return to Hull, but my friends spared no pains to stifle them. I might almost say that no pious parent ever laboured more to impress a beloved child with piety, than they did to give me a taste for the world and its diversions".

27. Entrance to the Dock, by Robert Thew, 1787, showing the lock gates at the entrance to Hull's first enclosed dock, which was opened in 1778.

28. Charlotte Street Hull, from a drawing by F.S.Smith, 1883.

The pleasures of society

As mentioned before, many of the merchant families of mid-eighteenth century Hull were still living in the town. By the last quarter of the century some of the most important of them had bought or built grand houses in the villages just outside Hull: the Wilberforces, Etheringtons and Broadleys in North Ferriby; two branches of the Sykes family in Kirk Ella and West Ella; the Peases at Hesslewood; and others in Cottingham, Melton, Anlaby and Hessle. And the less opulent began to move to the 'suburbs' - the gracious terraces of George Street and Charlotte Street just north of the new Dock opened in 1778. But even those who had villas outside Hull often spent the winter in their town houses. This concentration of well-off families created a lively social scene. Wilberforce, looking back, considered Hull:

> "as gay a place as could be found out of London. The theatres, balls, great suppers and card-parties were the delight of the principal families in the town. The usual dinner hour was two o'clock, and at six they met at sumptuous suppers".

William had to be more or less forced to attend his first play at the Theatre Royal, newly built for the famous actor-manager Tate Wilkinson. The company's repertoire was extensive: Shakespeare; comic opera; pantomimes; bawdy comedy - but any of these would have shocked a Methodist, for the theatre was altogether the Devil's work.

The balls referred to above were held at the Assembly Rooms built by public subscription in 1750 in Dagger Lane. (Earlier assemblies had been held in the upstairs room over the Grammar School.). The building is no longer there. We may imagine, however, that it was very much like the Beverley Assembly Rooms, built a decade later in the classical style, and containing a grand ballroom with pillars and glass chandeliers, a gallery for the orchestra, a card room on one side and a tea room on the other. Those who did not choose to dance could sit round and gossip with their

29. Sir Henry Etherington, in hunting regalia. Mayor of Hull in 1769 and 1785, died 1819. From the portrait in the possession of the Hull and East Yorkshire Hospitals NHS Trust.

friends and acquaintances or play a hand or two of cards. Both men and women would be fashionably and expensively dressed.

Assemblies were held regularly throughout the winter season, and attendance at these and other public events, such as Corporation dinners, would be interspersed with private dinners and parties. But the pleasures of life were not restricted to Hull. The social set to which the Wilberforce family belonged loved hunting and horse-racing and these pastimes took them out and about in the East Riding. Robert Broadley's diary and account book for the years 1768-1773[6] gives a vivid picture of the social life of which William Wilberforce would have been a part.

Robert Broadley, of Hull and North Ferriby was a young man whose life was dedicated to pleasure. From his monthly and annual accounts we see that horses played a very important part in his life; almost a third of his expenditure went on buying them, stabling them, riding them - the Driffield Hunt demanded regular subscriptions - and veterinary and shoeing expenses. Robert Broadley would often take short round trips, lasting three or four days, which might include assemblies at York, hunting at Driffield and Beverley races. In the summer he spent a fortnight at Scarborough to take the waters and bathe in the sea. Gaming and fashion were important to him and to his friends: he regularly owed sums of money for wagers lost; and he would bet on anything, including the sex of a friend's as yet unborn baby, and the weight of his favourite horse. He spent money regularly on clothes, often using friends to acquire items difficult to find locally - he records Abel Smith buying a hat for him in London; and on 28 October 1772 he "paid Mrs Wilberforce for 12 yards of narrow lace to set on Men's muslin ruffles".

The young William was immersed in this social whirl from the age of twelve. By the time he was sent to St. John's College, Cambridge, in October 1776, his religious fervour had quite disappeared and he had wholeheartedly acquired the "taste for the world and its diversions" which his family had encouraged.

University

At seventeen, William Wilberforce had become a popular and socially polished young man. He was witty, affectionate, high-spirited and not at all shy. He loved talking, and the exchange of ideas. (Ever since childhood he had been noticed for his beautiful speaking and singing voice). He was, and always would be, small and slight and, while not conventionally handsome - his nose was too long for his face - his features were lively

30. The Grandstand at Beverley Racecourse, erected 1767.

and attractive. On his first evening at Cambridge he was introduced by his tutor to a group of gambling, hard-drinking young men in whose company he spent most of his first year. Later in life he bitterly regretted the lack of social and educational guidance shown to him by his tutor.

By his second year he had found more respectable and sober friends; but he never managed to settle down to solid academic study. He loved visiting and entertaining, and his room was constantly full of friends coming and going, talking, making music, eating slices from the great Yorkshire pie he always kept for visitors. His friend Thomas Gisborne remembered late evenings:

> "My room and his were back to back, and often, when I was raking out my fire at ten o'clock, I heard his melodious voice calling aloud to me to come and sit with him before I went to bed. It was a dangerous thing to do, for his amusing conversation was sure to keep me up so late that I was behindhand the next morning."

In the holidays, too, William continued his socialising, travelling with his mother and sister and, in between, making the most of the balls and parties in Hull.

William did not do enough work to earn an honours degree, and was not interested in a life of scholarship. He left Cambridge in the summer of 1779 a very rich young man: his grandfather had died in 1774 and his childless uncle William in 1777 and the family money had come to him. In the usual course of events a young man in his position would either go on to take a working part in the family business or lead the young gentleman's life of leisure (typified by Robert Broadley). William Wilberforce chose neither of these alternatives. He began to plan a life in politics.

31. William Wilberforce, an undated sketch.

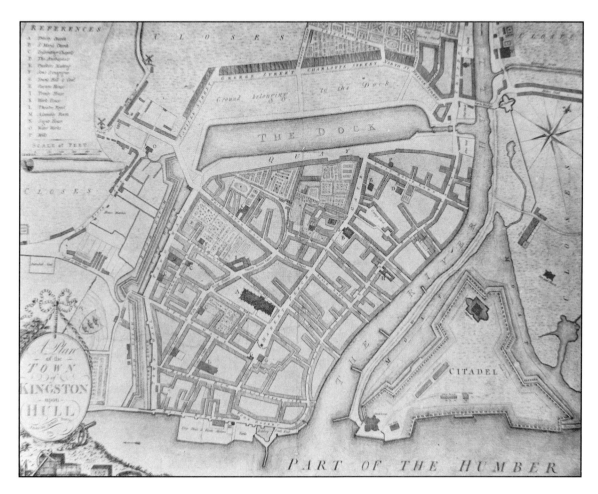

32. *The Town of Hull in 1784, from the plan by Robert Thew. This view shows the town as it was in the year that Wilberforce was first elected as MP for Yorkshire and was dedicated to him and his fellow MP Samuel Thornton. The major development since the time of Jeffreys' plan (fig. 3) has been the demolition of the old town walls along the northern side of the town to make way for Hull's first enclosed dock (known initially as the Dock, then Queen's Dock and now Queen's Gardens).*

Chapter 4

Early manhood and first seven years as MP

After leaving Cambridge, Wilberforce spent much of the winter of 1779-1780 in the gallery of the House of Commons watching the debates below. This was a smaller and more intimate chamber than the one we know today and it was the scene of great oratory: speakers competed to be the most brilliant, most stylish, most erudite, as well as the most persuasive. Instead of the confrontational and formal party system of today, the Members formed themselves into various groups and cliques. At that time, the only groups with any influence or power were varieties of the traditional Whig combination of aristocratic landowners and wealthy middle classes. The loose Tory coalition of Anglicans and country squires had lost political power and influence earlier in the century - although the sentiment and the tradition remained, and a Tory party revival, or rather a new version of it, was imminent.

Wilberforce often came across William Pitt in the gallery. He had known Pitt slightly at Cambridge; but now a close friendship developed between the two ambitious young men both aspiring to a political career. Although almost the same age - Pitt was four months older than Wilberforce - they were in many ways opposites. Pitt had a brilliant mind (he had gone to Cambridge at the precocious age of fourteen) and came from a political family: he was the second son of Lord Chatham (William Pitt the Elder), who had been a leading statesman until his death in 1778. Unlike his not very studious but gregarious and popular friend Wilberforce, Pitt was a shy, withdrawn, cold sort of man who found it difficult to make friends. He was not at ease in society, and was considered stiff and arrogant. Although so different from one another, he and Wilberforce formed a friendship which both valued deeply, and which lasted until Pitt's early death in 1806. Wilberforce helped Pitt to unbend; Pitt introduced Wilberforce to serious political ideas.

An election was not far away. Having decided to stand as a Member of Parliament for his home town, Wilberforce came back to Hull in the spring of 1780 to canvas support. Less than 10% of the population was entitled to vote; but those to whom the franchise extended - the freemen, or burgesses of the town - were not drawn just from the middle classes. Any man could become a freeman, by inheritance, apprenticeship, or straightforward purchase. Being a freeman at election time was of financial advantage because there was a universal system of payment for votes cast: the usual rate was two guineas a vote. Further expenses were incurred in bringing freemen living elsewhere back to Hull for the election. About three hundred freemen of Hull lived in London, beside the Thames, and Wilberforce practised his public speaking on them, at suppers he provided in the public houses of Wapping. Each freeman that promised to vote for him would have cost him £10 for travel in addition to the two guineas for the vote. (Inducements to vote were not only in cash: the candidate supporting the Government was able to promise jobs in Customs, an important consideration in a busy port like Hull). Wilberforce spent over £8000 altogether, a very large sum at that time. Later in life he condemned the corruption involved in becoming an MP but at the time it was accepted practice and Wilberforce did not question it.

There were three candidates for the 1780 election, two of whom were the sitting Members. Lord Robert Manners, an elderly general loyal to the Government, had been a Member for Hull for the previous thirty-three years and could depend on the votes of the Customs officers and the soldiers stationed in the garrison. David Hartley was the protégé of Sir George Savile, Governor of Hull, and of the Marquess of Rockingham, leader of the powerful Whig group of aristocratic Yorkshire landowners. He was not popular with Hull voters, perhaps because of his Catholic leanings. He was eccentric, dressed oddly, wore spectacles tied on by a band round his head instead of the socially acceptable eye-glass on a ribbon, and had a reputation for long and dreary speeches in the House of Commons. However, he must be remembered as having been the first Member of Parliament to bring the slave trade formally to the attention of the House of Commons: in 1776 he had introduced a debate on the theme 'that the slave trade is

33. David Hartley, MP for Hull 1774-80.

contrary to the laws of God and the rights of men'.

Because the timing of the election was uncertain, Wilberforce was worried that he might be disqualified as under-age. As it happened, his twenty-first birthday preceded the election by eighteen days. The party on 24 August to celebrate his majority must have brought him a few more votes: it was a grand affair, held in a field just outside the city walls and enjoyed by many of the townspeople of Hull, with a bonfire, a whole roasted ox and several hogshead of ale.

On 11 September 1780 Wilberforce received 1126 votes - exactly as many as the other two candidates managed between them. David Hartley was bottom of the poll with 453 votes, so Lord Robert Manners and William Wilberforce were returned as the two Members for Hull. How did Wilberforce achieve this success at the age of just twenty-one? It was probably a combination of the freshness of youth; a lot of money; an easy

A Copy of the POLL.

VOTERS NAMES.

☞ *The Persons whose Places of Residence are not mentioned live in* HULL.

Candidates.

A	Man.	Hart.	Wil.
ARchibald Callow, Gent. Ellerker	39		71
Ayrey Francis, Sail-maker		53	107
Anderson Andrew, Mariner	58		111
Atkin John, Block-maker	78	87	
Atkinson Thomas, Sail-maker, Thorne		89	160
Archer William, Cordwainer			188
Ainsley George, Mariner, Scarborough	120		231
Anderson Thomas, Cordwainer, Aukboro'	123		235
Allen Robert, Cordwainer, Patrington		124	237
Anderson Christopher, Clock-maker, Brigg	128		248
Atkinson Joseph, Stay-maker, Lincoln	129		249
Ayre William, Gent. Ellerker		141	267
Archer Thomas, Ship-wright	176		328
Ablet Thomas, Cooper, Drypool	195		369
Archer John, Mariner	212		406
Atkinson George, Cordwainer, Beverley		208	435
Ash Thomas, Custom-house Officer	251		478
Ainsworth Benjamin, Butcher	252		479
Anson Richard, Silk-dresser, Petticoat Lane, London		247	519
Andrew William, Labourer		253	541
Anfield Christopher, Joiner	293		559
Arnet John, Cordwainer	303		576
Allen Thomas, Yeoman, Patrington		267	591
Atkinson Thomas, Painter, Brigg	327		609
Author Francis, Blacksmith, Bridlington-Key			616

Atkinson

34. *The first page of the Hull Poll Book showing votes cast in the parliamentary election of 1780. The candidates were Lord Manners, David Hartley and William Wilberforce.*

and compelling public speaking manner; an attractive personality; and his popularity among the powerful merchant families who had seen him grow up and knew him so well. The merchants of Hull would be glad that one of their own would be there in the House of Commons to represent their financial interests.

The new boy

Pitt had contested the seat for Cambridge University at the general election, without success. But by January 1781 he was MP for Appleby, a seat obtained through the patronage of Sir William Lowther, and in fact made his maiden speech - a very impressive and universally acclaimed performance - before Wilberforce did. Wilberforce's first two recorded speeches were undistinguished, and were concerned with Hull matters: on 17 May 1781 he presented a petition from Hull opposed to the revenue laws; and on 5 December of the same year he contributed to a debate on the strength of the Navy by suggesting that the Navy should order more ships from Hull boatyards.

Although ambitious himself he was thoroughly pleased by the meteoric rise of his friend William Pitt. Pitt, always confident of his own worth, became Chancellor of the Exchequer in July 1782 and in December 1783 was asked by King George III to form a government. Prime Minister at the age of twenty-four, Pitt became leader of a new Tory party representing the interests of the country gentry and the merchant classes. His opponent was the great Whig, Charles James Fox, (hated by the King, who much preferred Pitt), who came to represent groups interested in reform - religious dissenters, philanthropists, industrialists and others. Although Pitt was his hero, Wilberforce did not always vote Tory. He was proud of being an independent member, and spoke and voted according to his conscience.

35. William Pitt the Younger.

36. Charles James Fox.

37. *The Polling*, by William Hogarth. From a set of four satirical engravings produced at the time of the parliamentary election of 1750.

Loosening of the ties

From his first days as an MP the gap between Wilberforce and Hull began to widen. London society welcomed him. He joined several gentlemen's clubs where he mixed freely and easily with the aristocracy, talked politics with the leading politicians, and gambled - though only briefly: he stopped when he realised that what he won others could not afford to lose. His favourite club was Goosetree's, where the membership consisted mainly of young men who had been his contemporaries at Cambridge. He was also welcomed into the houses of the rich and the high-born. He was well-off, he was charming and funny, and he was very popular at musical soirees: the Prince of Wales loved to hear him sing. He had rooms in London convenient for the clubs and for the House of Commons but he based himself at Lauriston House, left to him by his uncle William, on the south side of Wimbledon Common - the same house in which he had spent two years as a child. Pitt and other friends often used to travel out to Wimbledon in the evening and stay the night. There they could unwind and play the fool.

Even during the long parliamentary recesses Wilberforce did not spend much time in Hull. He rented a property at Rayrigg on the shores of Lake Windermere, where he sometimes roamed alone in the countryside but more often entertained visitors - his mother and sister Sally with Mrs Joseph Sykes and her daughter Marianne, London acquaintances, college friends and others:

"Boating, riding and continual parties ... fully occupied my time until I returned to London in the following autumn."

38. Thomas Thompson, (1754-1828).

Back in Hull, the man now in charge of Wilberforce and Smith was young Thomas Thompson. Abel Smith III had died in 1779 and Thompson, from lowly beginnings as the son of a small farmer out on the Holderness plain, had shown great talent from the moment he entered the counting house as a sixteen-year-old apprentice in 1770. He was highly thought of by the family and Wilberforce would have had no need to visit Hull in connection with the business.

Member for Yorkshire

In the first few months of 1784 Pitt was struggling against his unpopularity in Parliament. Wilberforce supported him in every way he could, speaking eloquently in the House of Commons and spending time with him in private. He began to plan a more ambitious way to help Pitt which would also further his own career. He would try to become one of the two County Members for Yorkshire, positions of power and prestige. On 25 March 1784 the freemen of Yorkshire were called to a meeting in the yard of York castle. The supporters of Pitt wanted to persuade the freemen to send the King an Address condemning the present ministry: a general election would favour their cause. The Whig lords expected to convince the crowd the other way. Wilberforce travelled up to York to speak. After five hours of speeches in rough and wintry weather the Whigs were winning the day and the crowds were drifting away. Wilberforce got up on the table, so small and slight that he was almost blown down by the wind, and in an hour of brilliant oratory (according to eye-witnesses including James Boswell), began to sway the crowd towards Pitt. Suddenly and dramatically, a messenger from London appeared with a letter - Parliament had been dissolved and a general election was imminent. The crowd roared its approval.

Wilberforce was feted that evening, but he had some way to go before securing the nomination for Yorkshire. He decided that he had better make sure of his Hull seat as a fallback. He set off the next evening and arrived in Hull at 2am the next morning, 27 March. He canvassed all day on the 29th and the 30th. The poll started on the 31st and lasted into the next morning. By the evening he and his cousin, Samuel Thornton, had been elected. But the people of Hull were not entirely happy: they knew that in a week's time he would resign his Hull seat if elected for Yorkshire. Anger was expressed in the form of snowballs and other missiles thrown at him as he was carried through the streets in his sedan chair. Wilberforce, however, was quick-witted and managed to turn the situation round. On reaching his mother's house - she still lived in the family house in High Street - he leapt out of his sedan chair, rushed upstairs and addressed the crowd from his old nursery window. He was so eloquent that he even managed to persuade them that he should choose his successor if he resigned.

That same evening, 1 April, he was on his way back to York for his nomination as candidate. Then followed four frantic days of canvassing all over Yorkshire, speaking at meetings in every sizeable town. Canvassing proved to both sides that the supporters of Pitt would win, and on 7 April the Whigs conceded defeat without a poll. Wilberforce was able to sign himself 'Knight of the Shire for the County of York.'

The 'great change'

Later the same year, in Scarborough with his mother and sister for the summer season, Wilberforce came across Isaac Milner, formerly usher at Hull Grammar School and now a clergyman and Cambridge tutor. Renewing acquaintance with him, Wilberforce found him to be good company: he was a large, loud, forthright man, an intellectual heavyweight. On the spur of the moment Wilberforce asked Milner if he would like to accompany him, his mother, his sister and his cousin on a prolonged continental tour. Milner accepted, and the party set off in two carriages on 20 October.

39. Isaac Milner.

The two men usually had one carriage to themselves: conversation turned to religion, and they read and discussed seriously and at length. Wilberforce at first ridiculed the Methodism he had once so keenly supported. But gradually Milner persuaded him to accept intellectually the biblical view of man's personal relationship with God. Wilberforce was called back to England in February 1785 to support Pitt's efforts to bring in parliamentary reform and he enthusiastically plunged again into London's social whirl. But in June he set off again with Milner on a leisurely journey across Europe, picking up the family on the way - and again they spent the days exploring religious ideas, reading the New Testament, and sorting out Wilberforce's various doubts and difficulties. This time he was emotionally as well as intellectually convinced. It seems to have been a classic conversion experience, profoundly changing his response to all aspects of life. Nowadays we might describe him as becoming a born-again Christian: Wilberforce himself called it the 'great change'.

By the end of October, still abroad, he was rising early every morning to pray and read the bible. He was tortured by his past sinful ways, which would inevitably, he believed, lead him down to eternal damnation. Back in Wimbledon a week or two later, he sank into a state of deep depression and began to believe that he must give up his present way of life altogether. Luckily there were friends around to dissuade him. Pitt, John Thornton, and especially an ex-slave trader turned Evangelical clergyman, John Newton, brought him to believe that he could serve God best by continuing in political life. His social life changed. He was still good company when visiting friends, but he avoided the theatre and parties, and too much food and wine. He resigned from the clubs. Above all he was looking out for the work God was calling him to do.

40. William Wilberforce at the age of 29, by John Rising.

Chapter 5

Wilberforce and slavery

The transatlantic slave trade was well-established by the middle of the eighteenth century. On the first leg of the voyage from the British ports of London, Bristol and Liverpool, ships left for the west coast of Africa with cargoes of cloth, iron bars, guns and alcohol. African chiefs sold their own prisoners, acquired in tribal wars and village raids, to the British traders in exchange for these goods. Then the African prisoners, men, women and children, were shipped across the Atlantic in terrible conditions, crammed horizontally in layers below decks, chained and left to lie in their own vomit as seasickness overtook them. This voyage, lasting seven weeks or more, was known as the 'middle passage'. When the ships reached the West Indies and the Americas the prisoners were sold as slaves, either to work on the sugar, rice, cotton and tobacco plantations, or as domestic servants. With the money from the sale of the African slaves the traders bought plantation products to take back to England on the third leg of this triangular voyage.

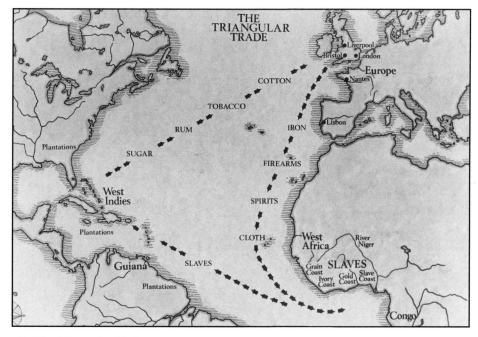

41. The Triangular Trade.

Long before Wilberforce took on the cause of the slaves there had been condemnations of the slave trade, first by the Quakers early in the century, then by John Wesley and his followers, among others. The first step towards abolition was taken by Granville Sharp, a government clerk, who campaigned on behalf of runaway slaves in this country. Mainly through his efforts to have the law changed, the Mansfield judgment in 1772 established the end of slavery in England.

In 1776 David Hartley, the Hull MP, moved a resolution against the slave trade in Parliament. In 1783 the Quakers formed a committee to work for the abolition of slavery and the slave trade and soon began to cooperate with Granville Sharp. Now, people with more power and influence were becoming interested. Sir Charles Middleton MP and his wife, Evangelicals and friends of Pitt, lived at Barham Court in Teston, the Kent village where the rector was James Ramsay. Ramsay had spent nineteen years in St. Kitts in the West Indies and had come back to England burning to fight the system of slavery that he had witnessed at first hand. Barham Court became a centre for the movement; and to Barham Court, in 1786, came Thomas Clarkson, probably the most important of all the abolitionists.

42. Scene on the West Coast of Africa, by Francois-Auguste Biard. The painting was presented to Sir Thomas Fowell Buxton to commemorate the abolition of slavery in 1833.

As an undergraduate at Cambridge Thomas Clarkson entered and won an essay competition on the subject of slavery. He began it as an academic exercise; but what he found out while researching the subject so horrified him that he determined to make it his life's work to abolish the slave trade and the institution of slavery itself. He published an extended version of his essay in 1786 and through this met the Middletons, Ramsay, Sharp and others. In May 1787, the Committee for the Effecting of the Abolition of the Slave Trade was founded, with Granville Sharp as chairman and Clarkson taking the lead. While the others all had other commitments the young, energetic Clarkson could devote his whole time to the cause.

Wilberforce joins the movement

Wilberforce had got to know the Middletons because of their shared interest in Evangelicalism and, since his conversion, he was seeing much of John Newton, the ex-slave trader. The talk was often of Africa, of the conditions of the slaves in the West Indies and of the slave trade itself. Wilberforce had moved back into London at Christmas 1786, selling the house in Wimbledon and buying the lease of number 4 Old Palace Yard, just round the corner from the House of Commons. Clarkson called on him here, first to leave a copy of his *Essay on Slavery*, and a second time to discuss it. The other abolitionists were well aware that they needed an influential voice in Parliament. Wilberforce had the right social connections and he was an orator who could hold his audience spellbound and who knew how to use emotion and reason equally skilfully. He was independent of party considerations. And he had the money and the moral inclination to throw himself into the fight. During 1787 they were sounding him out, and at the same time he was doing his own research into conditions in Africa and the West Indies. By the time Pitt asked him outright to take on the responsibility of being the abolitionists' spokesman in the House of Commons he was ready to commit himself wholeheartedly to the cause. This was obviously a momentous occasion for Wilberforce, for in later life he remembered the exact tree under which he and Pitt had been sitting at the time (see Fig.44).

43. Thomas Clarkson, portrait by A.E.Chalons. Clarkson is shown surrounded by some of the African goods which he used to demonstrate the skills and culture of the victims of the slave traders.

44. Group of clergymen at the Wilberforce Oak, Holwood Estate.

Getting started

The abolitionists had agreed that the abolition of the slave trade, rather than the institution of slavery itself, should be their first goal. While Wilberforce prepared to introduce the subject in Parliament Clarkson set off on a fact-finding tour of conditions in the slave ships in Bristol and Liverpool docks. This was a very practical investigation: he collected first hand reports from sailors; he took measurements of the holds where the slaves were crushed together in chains; he acquired examples of the instruments of torture - thumb-screws, forcible mouth-openers - which were sold in quayside shops; and he suffered physical attacks from irate defenders of the slave trade.

In the last days of 1787 Wilberforce gave notice in the House of Commons that in the next session he intended to introduce a motion on the subject of the slave trade. Fox and other Members assured him of their support. Wilberforce himself was optimistic at this point. He wrote to a friend:

> "the cause of our poor Africans goes on most prosperously. I trust there is little reason to doubt of the motion for the abolition of this horrid traffic being carried in parliament."

But the opposition was gathering its forces. Pitt decided that a Committee of the Privy Council should formally investigate the African slave trade: this would at least give public and official voice to the arguments for abolition. Unfortunately, it also had the effect of delaying discussion in Parliament. Wilberforce was working very hard preparing and gathering evidence. Too hard, perhaps, because he fell ill in February 1788 with a serious intestinal illness which lasted many weeks, causing one of his doctors to conclude:

> "That little fellow, with the calico guts, cannot possibly survive a twelve-month."[7]

Wilberforce himself thought he might be dying and begged Pitt to take on the slave trade question. Pitt replied promptly and kindly with a promise to do everything that Wilberforce would have done himself. This promise in itself might have helped Wilberforce to turn the corner back to health. The doctors prescribed opium. In those days opium was considered to be a normal and everyday medicine and it seems to have had a beneficial effect on his intestinal disorders; but he went on taking a daily dose for the rest of his life to ward off a recurrence of the illness. He must have been addicted, but he never increased his intake except temporarily when illness threatened, and he seems to have shown few ill effects in later life apart from trouble with his vision and a noticeable increase in absentmindedness.

Pitt moved that the House should investigate the slave trade (a vaguer motion than the one Wilberforce originally intended) on 9 May 1788; but a debate was not possible until the Privy Council was ready to report back. Wilberforce spent the next few months getting his strength up until his workload was back to normal. On 13 May 1789, using the Privy Council's Report as a basis, he made his first great speech for abolition, going into vivid detail about the miseries of the 'middle passage' and the brutalising effect of the trade on the Africans:

> "Does the king of Barbissin want brandy? He has only to send his troops, in the nighttime, to burn and desolate a village: the captives will serve as commodities that may be bartered with the British trader."

The tone of the speech, however, was moderate and unsensational. He went through his points one by one and he dealt with the arguments of opponents without allowing himself to paint them as monsters. And he was clever enough to appeal to their commercial sense as well as to their better nature. This is how the speech finished:

> "Sir, the nature and all the circumstances of this trade are now laid open to us; we can no longer plead ignorance, we cannot evade it, it is now an object placed before us, we cannot pass it; we may spurn it, we may kick it out of our way, but we cannot turn aside so as to avoid seeing it; for it is brought now so directly before our eyes that this House must decide, and must justify to all the world, and to their own consciences, the rectitude of the grounds and principles of their decision. ... Let not Parliament be the only body that is insensible to the principles of national justice. Let us make reparation to Africa, so far as we can, by establishing a trade upon true commercial principles, and we shall soon find the rectitude of our conduct rewarded by the benefits of a regular and a growing commerce."[8]

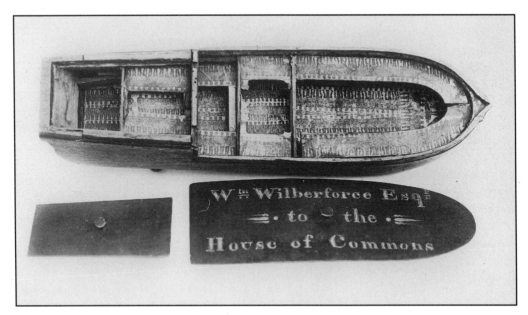

45. The Liverpool slave ship "Brooks". The model was exhibited by Wilberforce in parliament, to illustrate the method in which slaves were "stowed". On one voyage the vessel carried a total of 609 slaves (351 men, 127 women, 90 boys and 41 girls). It was normal for some 20% of the prisoners to die during the voyage.

46. William Pitt addressing the House of Commons on the French declaration of war 1793, by Karl Anton Hickel. Pitt is on his feet; Wilberforce is seated in front of the right-hand pillar. By permission of the National Portrait Gallery.

Pitt, Burke and Fox followed his speech with words of support. Unfortunately, at that point, with the House undecided, the debate was adjourned. By the time it was resumed nine days later the opponents of abolition had thought of a delaying tactic: they insisted that the evidence given to the Privy Council must be given again in the House of Commons so that the Members could hear it at first hand. Further discussion was put off until the next session.

The long struggle

So this first attempt at abolition failed, in spite of all the hard work and all the hopes of those concerned. From then on it was a long, long struggle to change the hearts and minds of the British people. (Detailed accounts of this long, hard campaign can be found in several of the excellent books listed in the bibliography). In Parliament Wilberforce led the battle, although he always had support from other prominent figures. In 1791 there was another debate which followed a similar course to that of 1789: those with financial interests in the slave trade defeated Wilberforce and his supporters by two to one. In 1792 Wilberforce, with Fox and Pitt, achieved a small step forward - the passing of an amendment "That the Slave trade ought to be gradually abolished".

But at this point international affairs had to take precedence. Louis XVI of France was executed in January 1793, three and a half years after the beginning of the French Revolution and the French Republic declared war on Britain a few days later. From then on the war with France monopolised the attention of the House of Commons. The war caused a temporary and very public rift between Wilberforce and Pitt in 1794 when Wilberforce voted against Pitt for peace with France, but the friendship was soon mended.

47. William Wilberforce, from an engraving published in Germany in 1795.

48. "Am I not a man and a brother" – the slogan of the campaign.

In 1796, 1798 and 1799 anti-slave trade bills were defeated again; but in 1804 another bill was actually passed in the House of Commons before meeting delay in the Lords. As abolition began to seem a reality, two of the main parliamentary protagonists died. William Pitt, the Prime Minister, Wilberforce's greatest friend, died in January 1806, brought low by the death of Nelson at the battle of Trafalgar and Napoleon's victory at Austerlitz. Charles James Fox, whom Wilberforce had come to like and respect for his fidelity to the abolitionist cause, died later the same year. It was not until the early morning of 24 February 1807 that the Bill for the Abolition of the Slave Trade received its second reading in the House of Commons and was finally passed by a majority of 283 to 16. Wilberforce received a standing ovation acknowledging his unceasing labours, over twenty years, on behalf of the African slaves. He was moved to tears.

It is important to remember, however, that during the whole of this period there was much effort going on outside Parliament. During Clarkson's fact-finding tour in 1787, he had encouraged opponents of slavery to set up local groups to campaign against the slave trade. He advised these groups to send petitions to Parliament, and petitions duly came in - from cities and towns all over the country. Public awareness of the cause was further aroused by the distribution of books and pamphlets written by members of the Committee, and by widely circulated popular poems by the philanthropist Hannah More and the poet William Cowper. The industrialist Josiah Wedgwood, a Quaker, produced a cameo - a picture of a slave in chains with the slogan, 'Am I not a Man and a Brother?' -

49. Olaudah Equiano. Captured by slave traders, he eventually bought his freedom and went on to play an important role in the campaign for abolition. He published his autobiography and toured the country (visiting Hull in 1792), and by his eloquence and erudition did much to promote the need for reform. From the painting at the Royal Albert Museum, by permission of Exeter City Council Museums and Art Galleries.

which became fashionable and appeared on many snuff boxes, ladies' bracelets and ornamental hairpins. As the years went by the campaign outside Parliament went on. The Committee was inactive for a period during the war with France but revived in 1804, Wilberforce, Clarkson and others still working closely together to gather and disseminate more and more evidence of the horrors of the slave trade. The triumph of 24 February 1807 was very much a shared triumph.

The Clapham community

Wilberforce worked tirelessly for twenty years - 1787-1807 - for the abolition of the slave trade. And yet this great cause was only a part, and sometimes a small part of his life in his thirties and forties. Inside Parliament his interests were wide and he spoke on many very different issues: international affairs, especially the war with France; the conditions of the poor; the Yorkshire woollen trade; cruelty to animals. More controversially, he was instrumental in the establishment of the repressive Combination Act in 1799 which denied to workmen the right to form trade unions. Outside Parliament he loved to get right away from the House of Commons to be with his friends in the country at Clapham.

50. Battersea Rise House, Clapham Common.

In 1792 he had been invited by his second cousin Henry Thornton, also an MP, to share a house with him on the west side of Clapham Common. This was Battersea Rise, a compact Queen Anne house to which Henry Thornton added wings each side for extra accommodation, and a library designed by William Pitt. Henry, like William Wilberforce, was the great grandson of the Hull merchant John Thornton; but his branch of the family had moved down to London earlier and had bought a large estate to the south of Clapham Common. (The John Thornton who gave young William extra pocket-money when he was visiting with his aunt Hannah was Henry's father).

The gardens of Battersea Rise were large and there was room there for Henry to build two more houses which he let to like-minded friends Charles Grant and Edward Eliot, Pitt's brother-in-law. Whether or not Henry Thornton had planned it, Clapham quickly became home to a colony of 'Saints', as they came to be nicknamed, all believers, most of them Evangelical, and all committed to good causes. In addition to those already mentioned, Granville Sharp already lived in the village; and soon two more fervent abolitionists, Zachary Macaulay who had been a plantation manager in the West Indies, and James Stephen, later to marry William's sister, both settled there. In 1793 John Venn, a great Evangelical preacher, joined the community as rector of the village church. Other like-minded friends were frequent visitors: Hannah More; Isaac Milner, now Dean of Carlisle; and Thomas Babington, Wilberforce's friend from Cambridge days.

The Clapham friends lived closely with each other. They would wander in and out of each others' houses, chatting, eating together, working constantly together to promote their many good causes. There was the slave trade, of course: but there was also great discussion about missionary activities abroad, resulting in the foundation of the Church Missionary Society in 1799 and the British and Foreign

Bible Society in 1804. The Sierra Leone project - the setting-up and the administration of a colony for freed slaves - took up much of their time. Nearer home there was an attempt at penal reform, for which Wilberforce worked closely with Jeremy Bentham. And Wilberforce also gave his support to the Society for Bettering the Condition and Increasing the Comforts of the Poor, known commonly as the Bettering Society.

As well as helping to organise, publicise and financially support these and many other charitable enterprises, Wilberforce was generous at a personal level. Like Henry Thornton he gave away a good part of his income - about a quarter, according to his sons. He was interested in the education of the poor and gave constant financial support to the schools for the poor run by Hannah More and her sisters. Like Wilberforce and most of her contemporaries, Hannah More believed that civilisation depended on the poor keeping to their appropriate place in society; so she instructed the pupils in the Bible and the catechism, and on weekdays they learnt "such coarse works as may fit them for servants. I allow of no writing for the poor"[9] she wrote to Wilberforce. He had annual subscriptions to all sorts of small charities, including some in his home town. The *Hull Advertiser* for the 2nd July 1796 has a list of subscriptions "for the purpose of giving occasional assistance to distressed Tradesmen of reputable character, by the loan of small sums". Wilberforce's name is high on the list with £52 10s. On the whole he preferred the recipients of his charity to be deserving, but he was often carried away by spontaneous generosity:

"Lent Robert Wells £13, which never expect again - he has a wife and six children to maintain, and ekes out a scanty income by a trade in old clothes."

Wilberforce's conversion had made him eager to put right what he saw as the lax moral climate of the time - indeed he wrote in his diary in October 1787:

"God Almighty has set before me two great objects, the suppression of the slave trade and the reformation of manners [i.e. morals]."

The aim of what became known as the Proclamation Society which he set up in late 1787 (and which later became the Society for the Suppression of Vice) was to clear up debauchery, drunkenness, profanity, lewdness and other immoral practices throughout society; but he appealed especially to the rich and powerful to set an example to the lower classes. This movement was not specifically religious. However Wilberforce's central desire was to share with others, especially family and close friends, his constant awareness of God's presence within him; and he was always on the lookout for the opportunity to bring his friends nearer to Christ. For example, before going out to dinner he used to plan topics of conversation which might lead on to deeper religious discussion. Surprisingly, this habit of prosetylizing did not make him an unpopular guest. Regardless of the subject of the conversation, he was always witty, amusing and vivacious. He began to write a little tract to explain his thoughts more fully to his friends, and this developed into the 491 pages of *A Practical*

51. Barbara Wilberforce aged 24, portrait by John Russell, 1801. By kind permission of the owners.

View of the Prevailing Religious system of Professed Christians in the Higher and Middle Classes in this country, contrasted with Real Christianity, published in 1797. It became very popular, had to be reprinted many times and is still read today. It was also instrumental in bringing him together with his future wife.

A new family

In February 1796 Henry Thornton married Marianne Sykes, Wilberforce's childhood friend from West Ella, near Hull. They were still close as adults and she had asked his advice about marrying Henry. Although very happy for his friends, Wilberforce was unsettled. He had spent several very happy years sharing Battersea Rise with Thornton; now he could only be a visitor. Over the winter of 1796-7 he started to express a wish to find a wife himself. He was thirty-seven years old and, although he had been briefly in love once or twice, nothing had come of these fleeting attachments.

His friend Thomas Babington knew of just the person for him - beautiful, dark-eyed, twenty-year-old Barbara Spooner of Bath, daughter of a rich banker, and a newly converted Evangelical. In April 1797 Babington engineered a meeting between them, ostensibly to discuss *A Practical View...* and Wilberforce fell immediately head over heels in love. His friends, slightly alarmed, tried to hold him back but he was completely besotted, and proposed to her on 23 April, eight days after they had first met. They were married in Bath five weeks later and spent part of the honeymoon visiting Hannah More and her sisters at Cheddar and inspecting their schools.

After the first polite enthusiasm, Wilberforce's friends did not much like the new Mrs Wilberforce. She was unable or unwilling to share or appreciate Wilberforce's political life: her only interests were her husband, her home and, later, her children. Here is a description of her by Marianne Thornton, Henry Thornton's daughter:

> "She was extremely handsome and in some ways very clever, but very deficient in common sense, a woman with narrow views and selfish aims, that is if selfishness can be so called when it took the shape of idolatry of her husband, and thinking everything in the world ought to give way to what she thought expedient for him. Instead of helping him forward in the great works which it appeared Providence had given him to do, she always considered she was hardly used when he left her side, and instead of making his home attractive to the crowds of superior people that he invited, her love of economy made her anything but a hospitable hostess."[10]

But William loved her dearly for the rest of his life. He may have recognised her faults but, as Marianne noticed, "he was always throwing his shield over her, bringing forward her best points and trying to persuade other people that if they knew her well they would value her more".[11]

The newly-wed couple soon moved into Broomfield Lodge, in the grounds of

Battersea Rise, now empty because of the early death of Edward Eliot. For the next decade they shared the idyllic family life of the Clapham community. All the couples were having children - the Macaulays, the Grants, the Thorntons; and the Wilberforces. Their first son, William, was born in July 1798. Barbara (1799), Elizabeth (1801), and Robert Isaac (1802) followed in quick succession, and then Samuel in 1805 and Henry in 1807. Wilberforce's widowed sister, married in 1800 to James Stephen and now with stepchildren, joined the Clapham community. The children of the various families, many of them inter-related, played together, sometimes with the black sons of Sierra Leone chiefs staying with Zachary Macaulay for an English education.

52. Broomfield Lodge, Clapham Common. From a photograph taken in 1904, shortly before the house was demolished.

The household at Broomfield sounds to have been rather eccentric. After family prayers in the morning the breakfast table was usually crowded with guests or friends who had just dropped by uninvited. The talk might be of a political, moral or cultural nature - but whatever the time of day Wilberforce was always ready to abandon the adults. Marianne Thornton remembered that:

"during the long and grave discussions that went on between him and my father and others, he was most thankful to refresh himself by throwing a ball or a bunch of flowers at me, or opening the glass door and going off with me for a race on the lawn 'to warm his feet'."[12]

The Wilberforces had many servants, but they were often inefficient and insubordinate. Wilberforce tended to employ people he felt sorry for rather than those who would serve him well. Although there were guests at most meals Barbara was a bad hostess, rather unwelcoming and economical with the portions. But visitors put up with the inadequate food for the sake of the company and the conversation at the Wilberforce table.

These were happy years for Wilberforce. He was surrounded with friends, he was working hard for abolition and other causes, he doted on his wife and he loved the company of his children, with whom he spent as much time as possible - playing with them, reading to them, taking them on little trips. But things had not been so happy for his family back in Hull.

> New London Sep'r 22d
> 1807
>
> My dear Sir
>
> The Hermit's kind Solicitude is soothed sooner than I expected. Mrs W. was this morn safely deliver'd of a Son & I thank God (indeed I ought) for my cup overflows with Blessings) both Mother & Infant appear at present to be doing as well as possible — I have a multitude of new Correspond.ts brought on me, by this Event in addit.n to a list before too long — Excuse therefore my hastening to subscribe myself w. real Esteem & regard
>
> yours very sincerely
>
> W Wilberforce
>
> I received the Chef d'Oeuvre

53. Letter from William Wilberforce to William Hayley dated 22 September 1807, announcing the birth of his son Henry.

News from Hull

His sister Sally's first marriage had been to widower Thomas Clarke, vicar at Holy Trinity Church since 1783. In the summer of 1797, the newly-married Wilberforces had been met on the road north, as they journeyed up to the Yorkshire constituency, with the news that Thomas Clarke had died suddenly at the age of forty-five. They immediately turned off to Hull and spent three weeks "cheering his aged mother and sorrowing sister." While he was there, Wilberforce persuaded Hull Corporation to give the vacant position at Holy Trinity to his former teacher Joseph Milner whose reputation was quite restored, Evangelicalism having by then become respectable. Unfortunately Milner died a few weeks afterwards.

Wilberforce found his mother fragile and ailing. In fact she had less that a year to live and in July 1798, Wilberforce was up in Hull again, this time for her funeral. She died where she had lived since her marriage, in the house on High Street. Wilberforce found this visit back to his childhood home very moving:

> "It was a solemn and affecting scene to me, yesterday evening, to be in my mothers room, and see the bed where I was born, and where my father and my mother died, and where she then lay in her coffin."

This was a short visit. On 6 July he arrived in his old house. Early next morning at 6 am he set out "with some little pomp" with the funeral procession to Beverley. Five hours later he was on his way home. Barbara was about to produce their first child and he was desperate to be back with her.

Even during this very brief visit Wilberforce would probably have called in briefly downstairs to catch up on what was happening in the business part of the house. Much had changed in the twenty years since Thomas Thompson had taken charge of Wilberforce & Smith. In 1787 the family firm had been joined in the premises by the bank of Abel Smith and Sons. (William Wilberforce was not a partner in the bank even though it was located in his house). In the same year Thompson had become a partner in both firms, and in 1791 the bank's name was changed to Smiths and Thompson. Thomas Thompson was becoming an important and respected figure in Hull and would go on to join Wilberforce in the House of Commons in 1807. When old Mrs Wilberforce died in 1798 he moved in to number 25 High Street with his wife and four young children and it became their home.

In 1800 Wilberforce's widowed sister, Sally, married James Stephen and moved to Clapham. From then on, with his mother dead and his old home occupied by another family, he had little reason to return to Hull. But he had not finished with the north of England. In 1807, fresh from the triumph of the abolition of the slave trade, he had a very important Yorkshire election to fight.

A LETTER

ON

THE ABOLITION

OF THE

SLAVE TRADE;

ADDRESSED TO THE

FREEHOLDERS AND OTHER INHABITANTS

OF

YORKSHIRE.

By W. WILBERFORCE, Esq.

" There is neither Greek nor Jew, circumcision nor uncircumcision, Barbarian, Scythian, bond nor free: but CHRIST is all, and in all. Put on therefore bowels of mercies, kindness," &c.—COL. iii. 11. 12.

" GOD hath made of one blood all nations of men, for to dwell on all the face of the earth."—ACTS xvii. 26.

54. Public letter from Wilberforce to the Freeholders of Yorkshire, 1807.

Chapter 6

The elder statesman

By 1807 Wilberforce had already been returned four times as Member of Parliament for Yorkshire after his first victory in 1784. Each of these elections had meant trips up to Yorkshire, to drum up support for himself, and also for his friends in Hull. In 1796, for example, he had spent some days there canvassing for Samuel Thornton (Henry Thornton's brother) and for Spencer Stanhope, the unpopular candidate he had imposed upon the Hull constituency when he chose, in 1784, to represent Yorkshire rather than his home town.

In previous elections, accommodations between candidates had meant that the contest for a seat did not go as far as a poll. This time, in the election of 1807, it was a fight to the finish. There were three candidates for the two seats. The Tory Henry Lascelles had been a Member of Parliament for Yorkshire since 1796 except for a brief absence when he conceded defeat in 1806 because of his unpopularity with the Yorkshire cloth industry. Viscount Milton, the young grandson of the great Whig Lord Rockingham, was put up by his father, Lord Fitzwilliam, as a Whig candidate to prevent Lascelles getting back in. Wilberforce, started as the favourite because of the immense respect and admiration he commanded throughout the country but especially in Yorkshire.

55. Wilberforce/Milton handbill from the election of 1807.

It was an exciting two-week battle, followed throughout the country in daily newspaper reports. Wilberforce's initial popularity fell when his supporters were justifiably accused of secretly liaising with Lascelles. On the third day of polling the running total put Milton in the lead. (In those days polling lasted for two weeks, sometimes more, and the only voting place for all Yorkshire was in the Castle yard at York). Wilberforce sent for his Clapham friends to help him in his campaign, but they were delayed on the way north because Fitzwilliam's well-organised election machine had ensured that all local and regional transport was engaged to ferry 'their' freeholders to York. Meanwhile Wilberforce supporters from the Hull area made their way to York by boat, farm wagon and even on donkeys. Thomas Thompson spent eighteen days in York, putting in long hours in committees and otherwise helping with the administration of his business partner's campaign.

It was a rowdy election campaign and enormous amounts of money were spent by the Whig and Tory candidates. Wilberforce was not rich enough to compete with their £100,000 each; but his supporters raised £70,000 by public subscription, of which only half was spent - many freeholders felt such loyalty to Wilberforce that they did not demand the usual free travel and subsidised bed and breakfast. In the first week in June Wilberforce scraped home at the top of the poll and returned to the House of Commons for his last stint as a Member for Yorkshire.

Wilberforce's career was at its peak. He was popular and held in high esteem both inside and outside Parliament; partly because of his role in the abolition of the slave trade, but also due to his reputation for honesty, moral integrity, and his transparent desire to do good and never to compromise his conscience. During the next four years he was as assiduous as ever, a good constituency MP and speaking often in the House on a variety of subjects both domestic and foreign - including the war with France, which he became less reluctant to support as Napoleon became more of a threat to the whole of Europe. In 1808 Wilberforce, still very involved with the Sierra Leone project, asked twenty-five year old Thomas Perronet Thompson, the son of Thomas Thompson of Hull, to be the Governor of this colony for freed slaves which had been set up in 1787, and governed for some years by Zachary Macaulay. (The colony was being handed over to the British Government to run but the Clapham Evangelicals, now nearly all in Parliament, still retained their influence). Unfortunately young Thompson, although full of reforming zeal, was not a diplomatic success. After two years he had to be recalled, and this caused embarrassment between Wilberforce and Thompson's parents.

56. *Thomas Perronet Thompson.*

Now Wilberforce was beginning to feel his age. The journey to and from Clapham seemed to him too far for daily travel into London; and, stuck in Old Palace Yard for most of the week, he was missing seeing his young children grow up. In 1808 he bought a house in Kensington Gore, a mile from Hyde Park Corner, on the site of what is now the Albert Hall. This gave him a little more time with his family. But his health, always poor, was proving troublesome. He began to develop a curvature of the spine which, as the years went by, caused one shoulder to drop and his head to fall forward towards his chest, and for which he had permanently to wear a steel and leather brace. This is how his friend, John Harford, described his attendance at a public meeting about abolition in 1814:

> "Mr Wilberforce was recognised as soon as he entered the room, and a lane was quickly formed for him to reach the platform. As we advanced the meeting began to cheer him; but for a few moments he was quite unconscious that he himself was the object of applause, for walking with his head inclined upon his breast he saw no one."[13]

By 1811 Wilberforce was seriously considering giving up his Yorkshire seat - industrialisation and the increasing pace of change had enormously increased the burden of his constituency business, and, in any case, he felt that his family still needed more of his time. Reluctantly, and after much discussion and advice from his friends, he resigned his Yorkshire seat in the autumn of 1812 and accepted the nomination for the pocket borough of Bramber in Sussex. His wife's rich cousin, Lord Calthorpe, owned most of the village and the thirty-six freeholders would do what he told them. The worthies of his home town of Hull called a meeting to mark the end of his Yorkshire connection:

> "In the October of that year [1812] a meeting of the freeholders of the county, resident in Hull and its vicinity, was held at the Mansion House to take into consideration the best means of testifying their respect and regard for him. This meeting voted a very complimentary address to Mr. Wilberforce, and, in proposing the address for the adoption of the assembly, D. Sykes Esq., beautifully observed that 'not all the blood stained wreaths of Napoleon; not all the laurels which graced the brow of a Wellington; not all the wreaths worn by distinguished statesmen, orators, wits, and poets, in every age - were equal (in the speaker's opinion) to the honour which Mr. Wilberforce had obtained by the abolition of the slave trade'."[14]

After 1812 Wilberforce was freed from most of the time-consuming constituency business; but from then on, until he left the House of Commons in 1825, he was constantly busy with a multitude of different projects into which he poured his still abundant energy and enthusiasm.

Still working for others

The Abolition of the Slave Trade Act of 1807 had made the trade illegal throughout the British Empire, but it had not by any means wiped out the entire trade. French, Portuguese and Spanish ships were still sailing the 'middle passage' with holds full of African prisoners, and even some British traders managed to get round the law by sailing under flags of convenience. Both

Clarkson and Wilberforce carried on, struggling year after year to clamp down on evasion of British law and to influence other nations. Clarkson travelled abroad, Wilberforce had meetings with leading foreign statesmen in London, including Tsar Alexander of Russia. Wilberforce encouraged the British Government to press for international abolition at the Congress of Vienna in 1814, but Spain and Portugal demanded a delay in enforcement. Napoleon, during his brief return to power in the same year, proclaimed the immediate abolition of the slave trade throughout France and the French colonies; but after the return of the monarchy there was no effective enforcement until 1831. Portugal and Spain moved towards partial abolition in return for financial aid from Britain. It was altogether a slow and unsatisfactory progression towards a complete end to the slave trade, and Wilberforce, in spite of constant letters and speeches in Parliament, was rather on the sidelines. Most of the business of abolition was conducted at meetings and congresses abroad, but Wilberforce's state of health did not permit frequent foreign travel.

In his mature years Wilberforce continued to support the many charitable and religious societies that he had been instrumental in setting up in his younger days, and to these he added others. By 1800 he was already voicing his disgust at the cruelty to animals so prevalent at the time; and in 1824 he was a founder member of the Society for the Prevention of Cruelty to Animals (now the RSPCA). As early as 1785 Wilberforce had supported Pitt in his attempts to achieve a moderate reform of the franchise and throughout his parliamentary career he kept returning to this subject. He disapproved of the way parliamentary seats could be bought and sold, although he himself was not unwilling to accept a seat under the old unreformed system. He also worked for many years for Catholic emancipation: although disliking Catholicism itself he realised that it was unfair, and even counter-productive, to deny Catholics the right to represent their community in Parliament.

He never lost his reforming zeal. He risked unpopularity with his landed friends by speaking out against the savage game laws, under which poachers were imprisoned, transported or even hung and he spoke often in the House in favour of bills to improve the working conditions of children in factories and up chimneys. He visited Newgate prison with Elizabeth Fry, whose work with female prisoners greatly impressed him; and in Parliament he supported those trying to secure better conditions in prisons and reform of the penal code.

For the whole of his adult life Wilberforce spent most of his time trying to improve the lot of those less fortunate than himself, both at home and abroad. And yet, in the last years of his parliamentary career, he was reviled by some of his contemporaries with accusations of repression and inhumanity towards his fellow countrymen, and his reputation has suffered ever since. Can these accusations be justified?

'A most consummate hypocrite'?

There is no doubt that Wilberforce was closely associated with many of the repressive measures enacted first during Pitt's time in power and then in the years of public unrest after the French wars. The harsh Combination Acts of 1799 and 1800, making trade unions illegal, ensured that masters had complete control of their workforce. The ancient common-law writ of Habeas Corpus (which prevented people being imprisoned without a proper legal process) was suspended in 1794 and again in 1817, both times with Wilberforce's open support. In 1815 he voted for the Corn Laws which prohibited the import of foreign corn until the price of British-grown corn reached a certain figure. This measure led to great misery and hunger among poor town-dwellers and Wilberforce, like other supporters of the Corn Bill, feared for his personal safety as rioting mobs roamed the streets. In fact 1815 was the start of five years of national economic distress, with a series of bad harvests. Growing discontent led to meetings and riots which were then followed by further and more repressive laws.

Perhaps the most well known of these riots is what became known as the Peterloo Massacre. On 16 August 1819 a great demonstration took place in Manchester, with about sixty thousand people gathering on St. Peter's Fields to demand parliamentary reform and the repeal of the Corn Laws. The crowd was peaceful and unarmed. But the authorities sent in a troop of armed cavalry, eleven people were killed, and several hundred injured. Public opinion throughout the country condemned this slaughter. But the Government of the day, under Lord Liverpool, retaliated by passing the punitive Six Acts which, among other measures, put a strict limit on public meetings and introduced punishments for the possession of blasphemous and seditious literature. Wilberforce, while deploring the loss of life on St. Peter's Fields, spoke in favour of the Acts.

Some radical and humanitarian reformers, both inside and outside Parliament - sometimes the same men on whom Wilberforce

57. Extracts from the Hull Advertiser of December 27 1800 and January 17 1801. Following near famine conditions in England in 1800, a government scheme to assist the poor by buying up stocks of herring caught in the Firth of Forth and then distributing them through the port of Hull to communities inland was enthusiastically supported by Hull Corporation, who appealed for contributions. £7000 was raised, with Wilberforce himself donating the huge sum of £500. This episode demonstrates his personal commitment to helping the poor and needy, although at the same time he was voting to ban the right of working people to improve their own conditions by forming trades unions.

depended for support in his anti-slavery endeavours - came to despise him for his repressive attitude towards the poor of his own country, especially because of the high moral tone of most of his utterances. He was accused of hypocrisy. How could someone who cared so much for the African slaves turn a blind eye to the slave-like conditions of the English labouring classes? The radical Francis Place called him 'an ugly epitome of the devil' and William Cobbett, the journalist, who had called him 'a most consummate hypocrite', regularly reviled him in his *Weekly Register*. James Boswell, so impressed when he first heard Wilberforce speak in York in 1784, circulated this verse:

"Go, W —— with narrow skull,
Go home and preach away at Hull.
No longer in the Senate cackle
In strains that suit the tabernacle;
I hate your little wittling sneer,
Your pert and self-sufficient leer.
Mischief to trade sits on your lip,
Insects will gnaw the noblest ship.
Go, W ——, begone, for shame,
Thou dwarf with big resounding name."[15]

Wilberforce cannot escape unscathed from these accusations. He was a man of his time, and like most others with his background he believed unquestioningly in the centuries-old structure of British society in which everyone, from the lowliest labourer to the highest-born aristocrat, knew his place and in which all contributed in their own way to the peace and prosperity of the nation. The poor worked hard - and, if they worked hard enough, could gain advantages which would enable them to climb the social ladder. The fortunate rich, like Wilberforce himself, had obligations and responsibilities towards the lower classes and it was their duty, in a personal capacity, to ameliorate the extreme poverty and harsh working conditions of the poor with whom they came in contact - usually by gifts of money. What Wilberforce could not countenance was any sort of radical change in the structure of society. Like most of his contemporaries he had been extremely alarmed by the revolution in France in the last years of the eighteenth century, and he was determined not to allow a similar revolution in his own country. His fear of a complete breakdown in law and order was what led him to support the repressive faction in Parliament. He did not see, or did not choose to see, that times were changing, and that the industrial revolution was bringing new injustices for which only the radical and humanitarian reformers had real answers.

There is no doubt that Wilberforce was a generous, kind and caring man who, like all his Clapham friends, unstintingly gave money and time to those less fortunate than himself. But although he would always respond to personal demands upon his sympathy he lacked the wider view that would have enabled him to see that the recipients of his personal charity - poverty-stricken labourers, struggling tradesmen, prisoners, country children without a chance of education and town children sent up chimneys - all these were representative of a working class which could only flourish with radical and wholesale reform.

This is the paradox. Wilberforce was unable or unwilling to see what was under his nose - the miserable repression suffered by the new industrial working class. And yet his passionate and lifelong espousal of the cause of the African slaves on the other side of the world helped to change history and gave him a permanent place in the story of human progress.

Retirement

In 1825, after nearly forty-five years as a Member of Parliament, Wilberforce retired at the age of sixty-five. He gave as his reasons ill-health, family commitments and the fact that the fight against slavery, his life's work, had been handed on to younger men. Two years later he said goodbye to Yorkshire with a six months' tour of the whole county, staying with various old friends and ending up at Wentworth House, the home of his old adversary Lord Fitzwilliam. In Huddersfield he met up with an elderly shopkeeper who came from Hull and remembered Wilberforce's wonderful twenty-first birthday party and the ox roast in the fields outside the town. During this extended Yorkshire tour Wilberforce included a visit to Hull - possibly the last before his death. Here, an article in the *Hull Packet* of 7 August 1827 records this festive occasion:

> "W. WILBERFORCE, Esq., – our respectable townsman visited Tuesday last, and paid his respects to the Mayor and such of the members of the Corporation as were present at the Guildhall; after which he traversed several of the streets, and in the afternoon proceeded to visit Drypool Church of which he is patron, accompanied by the Rev. H. Venn, the vicar [the son of John Venn, of Clapham]; the Rev. R. Temple, curate; and several of the respectable inhabitants. We understand he expressed himself highly gratified with the church, for the rebuilding and enlargement of which, in 1822, the parish was indebted to the liberality of Mr. Wilberforce and his friends. The party all visited the Sunday school adjoining, at present occupied as a day school, where he begged a holiday for the scholars, to their no small gratification, in which he appeared greatly to participate. The bells of Drypool church rang merrily in honour of the visit."

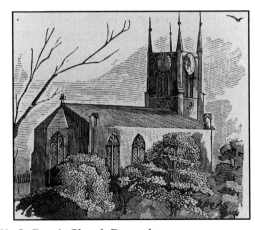

58. St Peter's Church Drypool.

Barbara was overjoyed when her husband retired. She was always worrying about his health. But their children continued to be both a joy and a burden. The first sadness had been the early death of their elder daughter, Barbara, in 1821. Robert Isaac, Samuel and Henry were a credit to their parents. All three went to Oriel College, Oxford; all three gained first class honours degrees; and all became clergymen. (Their father would not

59. Wilberforce and his family in the library of the Thornton's house at Battersea Rise. Sketch by Marianne Thornton, about 1824. By permission.

have been so pleased had he known that, after his death, both Robert Isaac and Henry forsook the Evangelicalism that had been so important to him, and ended up in the Roman Catholic Church.[16]) But the eldest son, William, was a continuing worry and brought financial disaster to his elderly parents.

The Wilberforces had decided to move right out of town after his retirement and, in 1825, bought a house and some land at Highwood Hill in the Middlesex countryside ten miles north of London. Here they lived a happy, busy and chaotic life, still with a constant stream of visitors and a host of infirm or disabled family retainers. The Wilberforces must have hoped to end their days at Highwood. Although Wilberforce had always given much of his income away he was careful with what remained, and had enough to see out his life and leave substantial portions to his wife and children. Unfortunately his son William, who had scraped into Cambridge University, left after two years under a cloud because of extravagance and drunkenness and, after a brief flirtation with a career in law, had taken up dairy farming with his father as financial backer. By 1829 the venture had failed and his father was financially ruined.

Wilberforce had to sell land in Beverley and Hull, and, worse, the family house in High Street where he had been born, where his mother and father had died and where the family business had flourished. Worse still, the old couple had to give up their home at Highwood, say goodbye to their servants and spend their last years going from one to the other of two of their clergyman sons, Robert Isaac and Samuel. Wilberforce said pathetically that what he would miss most was his books and his garden, and not being able to invite friends to dinner or to stay the night. But he always looked on the bright side. Here is part of a letter written on 24 September 1831 to Mrs D. Sykes of Kirkella, near Hull. (The original is in the Wilberforce House Museum). The address is Samuel's vicarage at Brightstone on the Isle of Wight:

"You and my dear friend will have heard of my having been compelled by my Eldest Son's Losses to retire from Highwood Hill that by reducing my establishment might be able to continue to make to my several children the annual allowances which are necessary for their comfortable maintenance. Mrs. W. and I are now enjoying a delightful Asylum under the Roof of my dear Son Samuel (my 3rd) where we have the gratification of witnessing his truly conscientious discharge of the duties of this pastoral Office. And I cannot but see the goodness of God in not bringing this stroke on me until my Children were educated [and] my Daughter married to a very worthy Clergyman ... "

[This daughter, Elizabeth (Lizzie), died in 1832: Wilberforce was distraught, but a little consoled by the infant granddaughter she left behind.]

Wilberforce never let go of the slavery question. Right from 1787, when the Committee for the Abolition of the Slave Trade was founded, emancipation - the end of the institution of slavery throughout all British-

60. "Soapy Sam" – Bishop Samuel Wilberforce 1805-73, third son of William Wilberforce.

owned territories - had always been the long-term aim although, during the decade after British abolition, that aim had been somewhat neglected. Abolitionists had hoped that the end of the trade in slaves would lead naturally to the end of slavery itself and it took some years for them to gather strength for a new initiative. About 1817 Wilberforce began to campaign for emancipation; but he knew that he was already too old and tired to play a prominent part in a new crusade. He handed on the leadership to a little-known young Member of Parliament, Thomas Fowell Buxton, a Quaker whom Wilberforce had got to know through a shared interest in prison reform.

Wilberforce spoke in favour of emancipation in the House of Commons in 1822, in 1823, and for the last time in 1824. But leaving the House did not mean entirely leaving public life. He occasionally chaired meetings of the new Anti-Slavery Society, and in 1830 he and Thomas Clarkson paid tribute to each other at a large Anti-Slavery meeting in London. His last public appearance was in Maidstone in April 1833, only four months before his death, when, with a weakened voice and failing body, he stood in front of a public meeting to present a petition against slavery. Popular opinion was now running strongly in favour of emancipation.

In spite of the loss of his fortune Wilberforce was happy in his last years. He was very proud of Robert Isaac and Samuel and loved staying with them and hearing them preach. When in the Isle of Wight he also had the company of his little grandchildren. He had always loved the company of children, and now there was a new generation for him to enjoy. In 1832 he wrote:

> " ... this house is enlivened by a delightful infant which twaddles about most captivatingly, and begins to lisp out papa and mama with more than Cicero's eloquence ... " [words typical of a doting grandpa].

He gradually grew weaker during the spring of 1833 and after two months at Bath, where the waters did not help his swollen limbs and various internal complaints, he was brought to London on 19 July to consult his doctor. During his last few days he was surrounded by his family, and old friends came to say goodbye. On Friday 26 July the Bill for the Abolition of Slavery passed its second reading in the House of Commons: and Wilberforce thanked his God from whom he had derived such comfort, guidance and constant support. Three days later he died.

61. Wax model, based on George Richmond's portrait of Wilberforce in the last year of his life. The model was presented to the City of Hull by Madame Tussaud's Waxworks in 1933, to mark the centenary of Wilberforce's death.

From the *Hull Advertiser* Tuesday August 16th 1833

FUNERAL OF MR. WILBERFORCE
... In accordance with the wishes of a large number of the most distinguished persons in the kingdom it was resolved to deposit his remains in Westminster Abbey. The funeral of this much lamented gentleman took place on Saturday, and nothing could exceed the anxiety that was manifested to pay respect to the eminent character which the deceased had during his long public life maintained. The procession, consisting of a hearse and six mourning coaches, and about fifty carriages of the nobility and gentry, left Cadogan Place at half-past twelve o'clock, and proceeded towards Westminster Abbey. A great number of members of both houses (about 430 commoners and 30 peers) arrived in the Abbey shortly after one o'clock. When the corpse and mourners arrived, a procession was formed at the great western door to the north transept of the Abbey, where the grave was; the choristers chaunted the funeral service written by Croft, and the the service for the dead was most impressively read by Dr. Halcombe. The supporters of the pall were, the Duke of Sussex, the Duke of Gloucester, the Marquis of Landsdowne, the Marquis of Westminster, the Lord Chancellor, the Earl of Clarendon, Lord Bexley, the Speaker of the House of Commons, the Right Hon. C. Grant, Sir R. Inglis, Mr Buxton and Mr W. Smith. Among the peers who walked in the procession were, the Duke of Wellington, the Archbishop of Canterbury, the Bishops of Chichester, London, Winchester and Hereford; the Earl of Rosslyn, Lord Althorp, Lord Aukland, the Earl of Denbigh, the Earl of Gosford, Lord Suffield, Lord Howden, etc. Amongst the distinguished members of the House of Commons were, Lord Althorp, Lord Morpeth, Sir Robert Peel, Sir James Graham, etc. The ceremony was not concluded until near three o'clock. Vast crowds of people attended in the Abbey and neighbourhood, and the ceremony was altogether of a most impressive kind.

62. Medallion produced in 1834 to commemorate the abolition of slavery within British colonies.

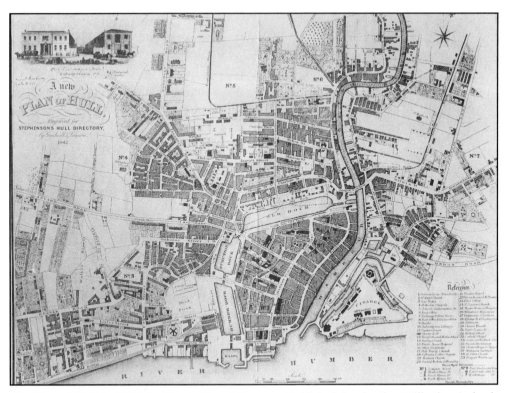

63. Plan of Hull in 1842, by Goodwill and Lawson. Published shortly after Wilberforce's death, this plan demonstrates the explosive growth of Hull which followed the breaching of the old town walls and the expansion into the surrounding territories of Myton (to the west), Sculcoates (to the north) and Drypool (to the east).

Chapter 7

Hull and its most illustrious son

The Wilberforce Monument

Although Wilberforce had not visited his native town for a number of years (the last documented visit seems to have been in 1827, see above), the reports of his death were greeted in Hull with an out-pouring of grief and calls went out immediately for some token of the town's esteem to be provided. A public meeting was held on 12 August and a number of worthy resolutions expressing the town's admiration of Wilberforce were passed: "this meeting contemplates with the warmest admiration the splendid career, during the period of half a century, of our late townsman William Wilberforce who, while he exhibited in private life all those virtues which spring from the cordial reception of Christian principles, in public life declined every scheme of personal aggrandisement"[17] and it was agreed that a monumental column, along the lines of Nelson's memorial in Trafalgar Square, would be a suitable form of commemoration, for "it would not be creditable to the character of the town, which justly glories in having been the birthplace of such a man, and in having first sent him into Parliament, to suffer him to sink into his grave without raising some lasting monument of its veneration and affection for his memory". A Memorial Committee was formed, a public subscription to meet the cost was launched, and the work was commissioned to be produced by the Leeds architect John Clark.

The statue on its column today dominates the eastern end of Queen's Gardens, but for most of its history it stood on Monument Bridge, at the south-western end of the present Gardens. Even this was not the site where it was originally intended to stand for Clark envisaged a waterfront location near Hull Pier, at the southern end of Queen Street near to the present site of the statue of William De La Pole. This option was ruled out on the grounds of cost, and Clark's second preference – the centre of Kingston Square – was also considered unsuitable, and so it was the third option – an open plot by St John's church, adjacent to the bridge leading into Whitefriargate – which was eventually chosen. This site was, and still is, an important focal point in Hull. It was at the junction of the two parts of the town – the Old Town within the walls and the new town which was rapidly expanding out from the old medieval core. The third of Hull's Town Docks, the Junction Dock (later known as Prince's Dock) had recently been opened and the monument was close to the site of Beverley Gate, where in 1642 the people of Hull had refused entry to King Charles I and so set in motion the chains of events which led to the English Civil War.

The laying of the column's foundation stone on 1 August 1834 was a great event in the town's history and is described by local histo-

64. Monument Bridge, Hull in 1866, showing the original location of the Wilberforce Column adjacent to St John's Church (now the site of the Ferens Art Gallery).

rian J.J. Sheahan in his history of Hull: "most of the shops in the town were closed, flags were streaming from the shipping, the bells pealed from the Churches, and a great assemblage collected to witness the proceedings"[18]. Not all the townsfolk were happy, however: John Greenwood, who was completing his *Picture of Hull* at the same time the monument was being erected, ends his text with the rather ungenerous statement that it "had been thought that the design, which is by Mr Clarke (sic) of Leeds, and the situation are unworthy the object"[19]. The work was completed some months later, when a statue of the Abolitionist was fixed at the top of the column on 12 November 1835.

Strangely, for a work which holds such an important place in Hull's civic landscape, the name of the actual sculptor of the statue is unclear. Contemporary accounts all refer to Clark as the designer of the column and to the firm of Myers & Wilson of Carr Lane as the builders but it appears that the inclusion of a statue on the top was not part of the original plan – perhaps being added in as work progressed to satisfy critics such as Greenwood. The only clue as to the identity of the artist seems to be an inscription discovered during the statue's move in 1935 which appears to read "Feort"[20], although no other works by an artist of this name are known locally. The work is in millstone grit and shows Wilberforce dressed in the robes of a senator, holding a scroll in his right hand.

The column is of the Doric order, set on a massive square pedestal whose faces bear the arms of the Wilberforce family, the Hull Trinity House, the Hull Dock Company and the Corporation of Hull. The base and col-

65. Wilberforce Column, view of the head of the statue.

umn together are some 90 feet (27 metres) high, with the statue adding another 12 feet (3.6 m.) to the overall height. A drinking fountain was incorporated into the base in June 1858, at the expense of Henry John Atkinson, Esq.

The monument stood in its original position for just a few months short of one hundred years and was the dominant feature of the Hull skyline. Its location, however, caused problems. Like many of the items of street furniture which decorated the town's landscape, the column was regarded by the providers of public transport as being an impediment to the flow of traffic rather than as an embellishment, and as in the case of a number of other statues (Andrew Marvell in Jameson Street, William De La Pole in King Edward Street) the needs of the Corporation's transport department took precedence and caused the monument to be moved.

A re-siting had first been proposed in the 1920s and was agreed upon late in 1932, when the programme of events in commemoration of the centenary of Wilberforce's death was being compiled. A major programme of redevelopment in the city's centre was underway with the infilling and landscaping of the Queen's Dock and so it was appropriate that the relocation of the column should be included as part of the new design. An initial proposal was that the column should be placed right in the very centre of the new gardens but eventually it was decided that the new site should be at the eastern end of the old dock.

The column was moved over a period of four months in the summer of 1935 and the entire costs of the operation (estimated at about £1500) were met by local builder Robert Greenwood Tarran. Tarran was the major supplier of building materials to the Hull Housing and Town Planning Committee and had recently been the subject of much unfavourable comment during an enquiry into the awarding of local contracts, so his generous gesture did much to restore his public standing; he eventually served with distinction as sheriff of Hull. Once the scaffolding had been erected, members of the public were allowed (for a donation of two shillings to the Mother Humber Fund) to make the ascent to the top of the column – at both the old location and, after the move, at the new location – and visitors were encouraged to leave their calling cards in a bronze container under the back of the statue. A ceremony of rededication was held on September 19 1935 at which Mrs Arnold Reckitt, a great granddaughter of the subject, presided[21].

66. *Wilberforce Column and Queen's Gardens viewed from Hull College in 1997. Photograph by Bill Marsden 1997.*

71

67. *W. Day Keyworth's statue of Wilberforce at its original location in the Hull Town Hall, drawn by F.S.Smith 1885.*

The Wilberforce Statue

Now situated in the garden at the front of Wilberforce House, the life-size ashlar statue of Wilberforce was originally designed to stand indoors, in the Hull Town Hall in Lowgate. The sculptor was William Day Keyworth the Younger and the work was completed in 1883, exactly 50 years after the death of its subject.

Keyworth (1843-1902) was the leading local sculptor of the later Victorian period and many of his other pieces (including Andrew Marvell, William and Michael de la Pole, Minerva in the Mandela Gardens and the Ferens Cricketer) still adorn the streets and interiors of Hull. His Wilberforce statue was presented to the town by Henry Briggs to commemorate the year (1881/2) that he served as sheriff of Hull, and was placed in the foyer of Cuthbert Brodrick's Town Hall. The unveiling ceremony was performed by the bishop of Newcastle (later of Chichester), the Right Rev. Ernest Roland Wilberforce, grandson of the subject, on 15 January 1884.

The statue was moved to its current position in the front garden of Wilberforce House in 1912.

Wilberforce House Museum

The last member of the family who lived at Wilberforce House was William's mother Elizabeth. It had always been a place of both business and residence and from 1787 the ground floor was used primarily as the premises of the Smiths & Thompson Bank and its sister firm of Wilberforce & Smith. The eld-

68. Smiths Bank, Whitefriargate, from a photograph published in 1903.

erly Mrs Wilberforce (who charged the bank a rent of £70 per annum) must have welcomed the appointment of one of the clerks as a live-in security guard following a bank robbery in 1785. After her death in July 1798 the businesses continued to occupy the ground floor and Thomas Thompson, the senior partner in both firms, moved in to the living accommodation upstairs. Thompson died in 1828 and the following year the bank (now renamed Smith Brothers & Co) moved to larger premises in Whitefriargate. In the April of 1830 the links between the house and the Wilberforce family were finally broken when William, with the greatest reluctance, was forced to sell the property to settle the debts of his son eldest William. Writing to Henry Thornton he said:

"... the house, in which I first drew my breath, though I cannot part with it without emotion, must with the premises be sold, and I am assured that I may hope to get from £5000 to £6000 for the whole"[22].

The purchasers were two local men; James Henwood, gentleman, and George Cookman, currier.

The story of Wilberforce House throughout the rest of the nineteenth century is one of neglect and gradual dilapidation. For a number of years the building continued to serve both as office and living accommodation. Henwood (whose portrait currently hangs the entrance hall) is said to have been the last resident but following his death the house was sold, in January 1855, to the Norman family. The demand for office premises in Hull's High Street was still high and the property, now numbered 25 High Street and known as Wilberforce Buildings, was increasingly subdivided to provide room for a number of different business. The story can be followed through local trade directories, which show that numerous firms connected with traditional Hull trades and activities such as Dobree & Co, Corn Merchants, Norwood & Co, Steam Ship Owners, and Lomas & Son, Seed Crushers and Oil Refiners, all shared office premises in the house.

The memory of the association between the house and its former illustrious occupant remained strong, and by the 1890s both local people and visitors to Hull were said to be constantly applying to be shown around the interior. Visitors, particularly those from America who called at the house as a place of pilgrimage, were, however, not always given the sort of welcome that they had hoped to receive and suggestions were made that the house should be taken into public ownership. The proposal did not meet with the approval of Hull Corporation, who were concerned about the costs of such an undertaking, and at one stage it was even proposed that the house should be dismantled and shipped to the USA.

For the fact that Wilberforce House is now owned by the people of the city of Hull we have to thank one individual, Councillor (later Alderman) John Brown. Brown (1850-1920) was a local businessman who succeeded his father as head of the highly respected printing and publishing firm of A.Brown & Sons and, on being elected as a member of the Town Council, made it his top priority to convince other less visionary members of the Corporation that it was their civic duty to rescue the house for posterity. It was an uphill struggle, for very few other towns in this period felt that their rate-payers' money should be put to such a use. Even more controversial

69. *Advertisement from Cook's Directory of Hull for 1897, when 25 High Street (Wilberforce House) was still used as business premises.*

were Brown's plans to set up a local telephone company, but here again the people of Hull have great reason to be grateful for Brown's pioneering work as Chairman of the Telephones Committee, where he was instrumental in founding the enterprise which is now known as Kingston Communications.

Brown began his campaign in 1896 with the publication of a pamphlet in which he argued that Stratford-on-Avon showed the house of Shakespeare and Edinburgh that of Knox, and that a museum at Wilberforce House could be funded by allowing some of the rooms to continue as offices for rent. He warned that, if the Corporation did not act, then a speculative developer could demolish the house to build new offices (a fate which had befallen many other High Street properties) and that if the authorities did not act they would "be blamed by the whole world now, and by all succeeding generations, so long as the fame of William Wilberforce shall endure".

From his position as Chairman of the Museum and Art Gallery Committee John Brown eventually saw his vision become a reality, although it was to be ten years before the Wilberforce House Museum was opened to the public and many hurdles had to be surmounted on the way. The campaign was waged primarily in the columns of the local newspapers and in 1901 received a major boost with the appointment of Tom Sheppard as Hull's first Curator of Museums. As well as the Wilberforce associations, much was made of the house's supposed connections with royalty, for it was thought at the time that King Charles I had stayed at the house for a night during his visit to Hull in 1639[23].

70. John Brown (1850-1920).

The property (including the warehousing to the rear) was finally acquired by the city in 1903[24], and work began to convert the house into a museum, under the supervision of the City Architect. A special rate was levied by the council to provide funds solely for the Wilberforce House restoration but part of the money was then put to other uses and so finance for the project was a problem; even in 1906 one of the rooms in the house was still in use as an office by a local firm and the premises at the rear continued to be used as a warehouse. Brown and Sheppard worked tirelessly to acquire objects and documents for display, and many local benefactors gave generously to ensure that the house would provide a fitting memorial.

On 24 August 1906, the anniversary of William Wilberforce's birth, Wilberforce House Museum was formally opened and dedicated to the use of the public. The opening ceremony was performed by Cecil George Savile, FSA, 4th Earl of Liverpool, in his capacity as a former president of the East Riding Antiquarian Society, and was witnessed by a "brilliant gathering" of dignitaries from the civic, business and antiquarian worlds, along with the American Consul and a number of representatives of the Wilberforce family. John Brown acted as host on behalf of the city of Hull.

The 1906 opening was only the beginning of the story of the development of Wilberforce House Museum. This is not the place for a full history of the building since that time but some highlights should be mentioned, in particular the reconstructed street which Tom Sheppard built in the warehouse at the rear of the house, only to see it go up in flames in World War II, and the sterling work of the Georgian Society for East Yorkshire (led by Rupert A. Alec-Smith) in rescuing period features from other buildings and their removal to Wilberforce House. The displays that can be seen at the House today are the result of a major programme of redesign and reinterpretation which was carried out by the staff of Hull Museums to commemorate the 150th anniversary of Wilberforce's death in 1983. These displays now occupy three of the first floor rooms, and cover the history of the slave trade, the story of its abolition and the life of Wilberforce, and include reconstructions of the interior of a slave ship and of a plantation slave hut. The reopening ceremony was performed by Richard Orme Wilberforce, Lord Wilberforce of the City and County of Kingston-upon-Hull, Chancellor of Hull University and great-great grandson of William Wilberforce.

The 1933 celebrations

71. 28 July 1933: crowds pack Queen Victoria Square for the events which marked the centenary of the death of Wilberforce. Photograph courtesy of the Hull Daily Mail.

The 100th anniversary of Wilberforce's death was commemorated in Hull by a series of events during the week 23 to 30 July 1933. Many members of the family visited the city, including Brigadier-General Sir Herbert W. Wilberforce, who laid the commemoration stone for the new premises of the Hull Grammar School in Bricknell Avenue. The celebrations began on the 23rd with a procession from the Guildhall past Wilberforce House and the Old Grammar School to Holy Trinity Church. Exhibitions were held at the

City Hall and the Central Library and included the first showing in Hull of the wax model of Wilberforce which was donated to the city by Madame Tussaud's. The organisers were keen to involve representations of the black community: the guide at the City Hall was a freed slave and recitals of 'negro spirituals, sketches, etc were given by coloured artists, whose sympathetic renderings delighted their hearers'. The civic reception and dinner on the 24th was addressed by Dr. Harold A. Moody, 'President of the League of Coloured Peoples', and the week culminated in a great public rally in Queen Victoria Square on 28 July.

Twinning with Freetown

Hull is proud of its connections with Sierra Leone, which go back over more than two centuries. Following the abolition of the slave trade in 1807, the Crown Colony became the home of many Africans who had rescued by the British from the ships of nations who continued to trade in slaves, and settlement gradually spread inland from Freetown. The country became independent in 1961, as a member of the British Commonwealth, and became a republic in 1971, with Siaka Stevens (who retired 1985) as the first President.

In 1982, at the request of the government of Sierra Leone, its capital Freetown and Hull were united as twin towns. In October of that year a civic delegation led by Lord Mayor Councillor Alex Clarke paid a seven-day visit to West Africa to seal the arrangements. According to newspaper reports the members of the Hull party were given a rapturous reception wherever they travelled and were treated as a full state delegation. Since then the two cities have both benefited from their relationship in trade, cultural and educational terms. Hull first marked the connection by choosing the name "Freetown Court" for a newly-built block of student flats on Endike Lane (formally opened by Victor E Sumner, High Commissioner for Sierra Leone in 1982) and then chose the name Freetown Way for the city's northern inner-city link road (opened by High Commissioner Sumner in 1986).

The ties were strengthened when a civic party led by Lord Mayor Councillor Alf Bowd visited Sierra Leone in May 1987 to attend the celebrations for the 200th anniversary of the founding of Freetown, and on this occasion presented to the Freetown City Council a bust of Wilberforce, the work of Hull sculptor Kevin Storch (Fig 72).

The people of Hull have also helped the people of their twin town in other ways. The Hull Freetown Society was established, and in late 1989 sent a collection of over 57,000 books to Sierra Leone. In 1990 local parishes of the Catholic Church took the lead in raising a considerable amount of money to help improve sanitation and water supply as part of the Water Aid appeal, and in 1992 supplies were collected for the benefit of the Connaught Hospital at Freetown.

The Wilberforce Lecture

The city of Kingston upon Hull continues to honour its most illustrious son and since 1995 has hosted an occasional series of lectures at which internationally-known cam-

72. *Presentation at Freetown City Hall, May 1987. Photograph kindly supplied by Barbara Robinson.*

73. *Paul Robeson, the distinguished American performer and civil rights activist, was invited to Hull as part of the events to mark the centenary of the birth of Wilberforce. He gave a gala concert in the City Hall on 24 April 1960 and afterwards visited Wilberforce House.*

paigners are invited to speak on their work in combating the abuse of human rights. The Lecture is accompanied by the presentation of the Wilberforce Medallion to an individual who has made an outstanding contribution to the furtherance of human rights. The first Wilberforce Lecture was given by Hugh O'Shaughnessy, formerly Foreign Correspondent with *The Observer*, who was one of the first journalists to draw attention to the genocide in East Timor. 1996 saw the award of the Wilberforce Medallion to Aung San Suu Kyi, the elected leader of Burma, who was imprisoned by the military dictatorship of her country. In 1997 the Medallion was awarded posthumously to Ken Saro-Wiwa, the martyred leader of the Ogoni people of Nigeria, and on this occasion the Wilberforce Lecture was given by Professor Wole Soyinka, the Nigerian novelist and Nobel Laureate. The 1998 award was to Dr. Alex-Anthony Williams for his work in running the Famcare Medical Centre at Freetown, despite the chaos which erupted following the 1997 military coup in Sierra Leone.

The 1999 Wilberforce Lecture, held on Friday 4 June, was the highlight of the celebrations that marked the 700th anniversary of the awarding of Hull's first town charter, and was a special day in Hull's history. The speaker was Archbishop Emeritus Desmond Tutu, who spoke of the crippling burden of Third World debt, and also the debt that those who value human rights owe to William Wilberforce. At an open air celebration in Queens Gardens presided over by the Lord Mayor Brian Wilkinson, the Archbishop attempted and eventually succeeded in getting the city's dignitaries – including Wilberforce's successors as MPs for Hull Kevin McNamara, Alan Johnson and John Prescott - to join in the South African-style arm-waving and chanting in a celebration of freedom. What would William Wilberforce have made of it all?

74. *Archbishop Desmond Tutu at the Wilberforce Monument, 1 February 1989. Picture by Anthony David Baynes.*

75. *Archbishop Emeritus Desmond Tutu and the Wilberforce Lecture, Queen's Gardens, 4 June 1999. Photograph by Eddie Rolmanis.*

Notes

1. quoted in: CROWTHER, *Descriptions of East Yorkshire: De La Pryme to Head.* E.Y.L.H.S., 1992, p.16.

2. Under the turnpiking system, travellers paid tolls which enabled local turnpike trusts - run by local landowners, merchants and town corporations - to improve and repair heavily-used sections of the public highway.

3. quoted in: WOODWARD, *Descriptions of East Yorkshire: Leland to Defoe.* E.Y.L.H.S., 1985, p.56.

4. East Riding of Yorkshire Archives and Record Service: DDHB 35/61 *Will of Robert Wilberforce, 1764.*

5. This, and all otherwise unattributed quotations, are taken from the *Life of William Wilberforce* by Robert Isaac and Samuel Wilberforce, which contains first-hand accounts from William Wilberforce's diaries, letters and conversations as well as biographical details and anecdotes contributed by friends and family.

6. University of Hull Brynmor Jones Library, Archives and Special Collections: DP/146 *Diary and account book of Robert Broadley 1768-1775.*

7. HARFORD, *Recollections of William Wilberforce Esq.* Longman, 1864, p.90.

8. This speech is reproduced in: *Crowned Masterpieces of Eloquence.* International Library Society, 1919, Section 3, pp.424-431.

9. quoted in the *Dictionary of National Biography*, vol. 38, p.417

10. quoted in FORSTER, *Marianne Thornton 1797-1887.* Edward Arnold, 1956, pp.42-3.

11. quoted in FORSTER, p.44.

12. quoted in: POLLOCK, *Wilberforce.* Constable, 1977, p.183.

13. HARFORD, p.57.

14. SHEAHAN, *History of the Town and Port of Kingston upon Hull.* 2nd ed. 1866, p.674.

15. quoted in FURNEAUX, *William Wilberforce.* Hamish Hamilton, 1974, p.283.

16. Robert Isaac Wilberforce was Rector of Burton Agnes and Archdeacon of the East Riding when he became a Roman Catholic in 1854. Samuel became successively bishop of Oxford and Winchester.

17. This and the following quotation are from SHEAHAN, pp.672-3.

18. SHEAHAN p.673.

19. GREENWOOD, *Picture of Hull*, 1835, p.189.

20. A reference to the name Feort as the possible sculptor comes from an article published in the John Humber column of the Hull Daily Mail on 15 April 1935: the columnist, who had taken the opportunity to climb the scaffolding to the top of the monument prior to its move to Queen's Gardens, stated that he saw the name Feort and the date 1835 carved on the bottom of the statue's skirt.

21. We are particularly grateful to Chris Ketchell of the Hull Local History Unit for information about the column and its 1935 move. Chris's typescript notes include much valuable information from Mr Alf Turner, who was an employee of Tarran's at the time the column was moved.

22. Quoted in RUTHERFORD, *History of Wilberforce House*.

23. The much-repeated story that King Charles I lodged with Sir John Lister at the house now known at Wilberforce House during his visit to Hull in 1639 has been conclusively demonstrated to be false by David Neave in his study of the work of William Catlyn (the House's architect), published in 1996.

24. The deed of conveyance is dated 15 April 1903. The vendors were Harrison Holt and John Bouch Willows, seed crushers of Hull, and the purchase price was £4500: Hull Guildhall Modern Records, ref. 1545 (Wilberforce House Deeds).

Works consulted

Manuscript and newspaper sources

EAST RIDING OF YORKSHIRE ARCHIVE AND RECORDS SERVICE
DDHB 35/61 A copy of the will of Robert Wilberforce, 1764.
Parish Registers: Hull St Mary's Lowgate, Hull Trinity, Beverley St Mary's.

HULL CITY ARCHIVES
DFS\W (Box 3): W.Foot Walker, notes on Hull Sculptors.
HULL CITY COUNCIL MODERN RECORDS
Wilberforce House Deeds, ref. 1545.

HULL LOCAL HISTORY UNIT
Wilberforce Monument (typescript), C.Ketchell, September 1993.
William Wilberforce Again (typescript), C.Ketchell, 1st October 1993.
Hull's Men of Stone: the Keyworths (typescript), C.Ketchell, April 2000.

HULL LOCAL STUDIES LIBRARY.
Hull and East Riding Graphic.
The Hull Advertiser.
The Hull Daily Mail.
The Hull Packet.
A small collection of autographed Wilberforce letters.
Collection of maps and plans.
Trade Directories.

UNIVERSITY OF HULL BRYNMOR JONES LIBRARY
(ARCHIVES AND SPECIAL COLLECTIONS)
DP/146 Diary and account book of Robert Broadley 1768-1773.

WILBERFORCE HOUSE MUSEUM
Letter from William Wilberforce to Mrs D. Sykes of Kirkella, 24 September 1831.
Wilberforce Archive: Boxes 3, 5 and 21 (Images).

Books and articles

ALDRIDGE, Carolyn, *Images of "Victorian" Hull: F.S. Smith's Drawings of the Old Town*. Hull City Museums & Art Galleries and the Hutton Press, 1989.
ALEC-SMITH, R.A., Wilberforce House, Hull. *Country Life*, March 30 1951.
ALLISON, K.J. ed., *A History of the County of York, East Riding: volume I, the City of Kingston upon Hull* (Victoria County History series). OUP, 1969.
ALLISON, K.J., *'Hull Gent. Seeks Country Residence' 1750-1850*. East Yorkshire Local History Society, 1981.
BROWN, John, *Wilberforce House, High Street, Hull: A Memoir and a Memorial*. Privately published June 1896. New edition published 1985 as Malet Lambert Local History Reprints No.36.
BULMAN, D.J. and Eastcrabbe, A., *North Ferriby: A Villagers' History*. Lockington Publishing Co., North Ferriby, 1982.
BURKE'S LANDED GENTRY, 18th edition, volume 3. Burke's Peerage Limited, London, 1972.
CASSELL'S HISTORY OF ENGLAND, Cassell and Company Limited, London, 1905.
COLBECK, Maurice, *Yorkshire History Makers*. EP Publishing Ltd., 1976.
CROWNED MASTERPIECES OF ELOQUENCE. 3 vols. International University Society, 1919.
CROWTHER, Jan, ed., *Descriptions of East Yorkshire: De la Pryme to Head*. East Yorkshire Local History Society, 1992.
DICTIONARY OF NATIONAL BIOGRAPHY, edited by Leslie Stephen. Smith, Elder and Co., 1885-1912.
EASTON, H.T., *The History of a Banking House*. Blades, East and Blades, London, 1903.
FLEMING, David, *Survival! 400 years of Hull's Old Grammar School*. Hull City Museums and Art Galleries, 1988.
FORSTER, E.M., *Marianne Thornton 1797-1887: a Domestic Biography*. Edward Arnold, 1956.
FURNEAUX, Robin, *William Wilberforce*. Hamish Hamilton, 1974.
GENT, Thomas, *Annales Regioduni Hulluni; or, the history of the royal and beautiful town of Kingston upon Hull*. Hull, 1735.
GIFFORD, Zerbanoo, *Thomas Clarkson and the Campaign against Slavery*. Anti-Slavery International, 1996.
GILLETT, Edward and MacMAHON, Kenneth A., *A History of Hull*, 2nd Edition. Hull University Press 1989.
GREENWOOD, John, *Picture of Hull*. Greenwood, Hull, 1835.
FAY, J.B., *Wilberforce House: Its History and Collections*. Hull, 1949.
HALL, Ivan and Elizabeth, *Georgian Hull*. York: Ebor Press, 1978.
HARFORD, John, *Recollections of William Wilberforce Esq*. Longman, 1864.
HATT, Christine, *Slavery from Africa to the Americas* (History in Writing series). Evans Brothers Ltd, 1997.
HULL GRAMMAR SCHOOL, *The City and The School* (essays published in commemoration of the 500th anniversary of the endowment of the Grammar School of Kingston upon Hull). Hull, 1979.
JACKSON, Gordon, *Hull in the Eighteenth Century: a Study in Economic and Social History*. OUP, 1972.
JACKSON, Gordon, *The Trade and Shipping of Eighteenth Century Hull*. East Yorkshire Local History Society, 1975.

LAWSON, John, *A Town Grammar School through Six Centuries.* OUP, 1963.
LEAN, Garth, *God's Politician.* Darton, Longman and Todd Ltd., 1980.
LEAS, Allan, *The Abolition of the Slave Trade.* Batsford, 1989.
MARKHAM, John, *Nineteenth-century parliamentary elections in East Yorkshire.* East Yorkshire Local History Society, 1982.
NEAVE, David, Artisan Mannerism in North Lincolnshire and East Yorkshire: the work of William Catlyn (1628-1709) of Hull, in *Lincolnshire People and Places: Essays in Memory of Terence R. Leach (1937-1994),* ed. Christopher Sturman. The Society for Lincolnshire History and Archaeology, Lincoln, 1996.
NEW ENCYCLOPAEDIA BRITANNICA. 15th ed., 1997.
OLIVER, George, *The History and Antiquities of the Town and Minster of Beverley.* Beverley, 1829.
POLLOCK, John, *Wilberforce.* Constable, 1977.
POULSON, George, *Beverlac: or, the antiquities and history of the town of Beverley.* Beverley, 1829.
ROBINSON, Arthur R.B., *The Counting House: Thomas Thompson of Hull (1754-1828) and his family.* York: Ebor Press, 1992.
RUTHERFORD, Ian, *History of Wilberforce House.* Hull City Museums and Art Galleries, n.d.
SHEAHAN, J.J., *History of the Town and Port of Kingston-upon-Hull.* 2nd ed. Beverley: John Green, 1866.
SHEPPARD, T., *Wilberforce House: Its History and Collections* (new edition) Hull, 1927.
SHEPPARD, Thomas, *William Wilberforce. Dedication of his Birthplace to the Public.* Hull Museums Publication No.34, 1906. New edition published 1983 as Malet Lambert Local History Reprints (Extra Volume) No.50.
SHEPPARD, Thomas, *William Wilberforce of Hull,* and *The Wilberforce Centenary* in Hull Museum Publication No.181 (Record of Additions, 1933), being reprints from *"Ours",* the magazine of Reckitt & Sons Ltd.
SMITH, E.A., 'The Yorkshire Elections of 1806 and 1807: a Study in Electoral Management', *Northern History,* vol 2, 1967.
STRONG, Roy, *The Story of Britain.* Hutchinson, 1996.
THOMAS, Hugh, *The Slave Trade: the History of the Atlantic Slave Trade 1440-1870.* Picador, 1997.
THORNE, R.G., *The House of Commons 1790-1829* (History of Parliament series). 5 vols. Secker and Warburg, 1986.
TICKELL, John, *The History of the Town and County of Kingston upon Hull.* Hull, 1st edition. Hull, 1796.
WARNER, Oliver, *William Wilberforce and his Times.* Batsford, 1962.
WILBERFORCE, Robert Isaac and Samuel, *The Life of William Wilberforce, in five volumes.* John Murray, 1838.
WILDRIDGE, T.Tindall, *Old and New Hull.* Peck & Son, Hull 1884; Supplementary edition 1889.
WILDRIDGE, T.Tindall, *The Wilberforce Souvenir.* Peck & Son, Hull, 1884.
WOODWARD, Donald, *Descriptions of East Yorkshire: Leland to Defoe.* East Yorkshire Family History Society, 1985.
WRANGHAM, C.E., ed., *Journey to the Lake District from Cambridge 1779: a diary written by William Wilberforce.* Oriel Press, 1983.

List of illustrations

Cover:

View of the market place at Kingston upon Hull by Thomas Malton the Younger, 1780 (Hull City Council, Ferens Art Gallery).

William Wilberforce by Karl Hickel, 1794 (Hull City Council, Wilberforce House Museum).

Chapters 1-7

1 "Kyngeston upon Hull" in 1640 by Wenceslaus Hollar. From Sheahan's *History of Hull*, 1866.

2 Beverley Gate. From Tickell's *History of Hull*, 1796.

3 Plan of Hull c.1770. From Thomas Jeffreys' *Plan of the county of York*, published 1775 (Hull City Council, Local Studies Library).

4 The East Riding of Yorkshire in 1610. From John Speed's *Plan of the North and East Ridins* (sic), published 1611-12 (Hull City Council, Local Studies Library).

5 Hull Sugar House. From a plan in *Gent's History of Hull*, 1735.

6 Descendants of Alderman William Wilberforce. Sources: parish registers for Hull Holy Trinity, Hull St. Mary, Beverley St. Mary; Monumental inscriptions for Beverley St. Mary; Burke 1972; Pollock 1977; IGI.

7 St Mary's Lowgate, Hull. From Tickell's *History of Hull*, 1796.

8 Wilberforce House in 1835. Drawn by John Greenwood and published in his *Picture of Hull*.

9 Wilberforce House, the staircase and Venetian window (Hull City Council, Wilberforce House Museum).

10 Wilberforce House, view of the stairwell ceiling (Hull City Council, Wilberforce House Museum).

11 The "Georgian Houses", 23-24 High Street. Photograph by Bill Marsden 1997 (Hull City Council, Local Studies Library).

12 Wilberforce House, the nursery. From a drawing by T.Tindall Wildridge published in his *Old and New Hull*, 1884.

13 The Font at Hull Holy Trinity Church. From T.Tindall Wildridge's *Old and New Hull*, 1884.

14 Aston Hall North Ferriby. Drawing by Suzy Luck. First published in *North Ferriby: a Villagers' History*, by D.J.Bulman and A.Eastcrabbe (North Ferriby 1982).

15 Hull Grammar School. Drawn by John Greenwood and published in his *Picture of Hull*, 1835.

16 179 High Street Hull. From a drawing by F.S.Smith dated 1887 (Hull City Council, Wilberforce House Museum).

17 "King Billy". From Tickell's *History of Hull*, 1796.

18 The old Hull Guildhall and Prison. From a painting by Benjamin Gale c.1780 (Hull City Council, Ferens Art Gallery).

19 Hull Holy Trinity Church. From Tickell's *History of Hull*, 1796.

20 William Wilberforce in his twelfth year (1770), after John Russell. By kind permission of the Trustees of the late C.E.Wrangham.

21 St Mary's church, Beverley. From Poulson's *History of Beverley*, 1829.

22 Abel Smith II. From H.T.Easton's *History of a Banking House*, 1903.

23 William Wilberforce and Hannah Thornton, portrait by Joseph Highmore; presumed to have been painted at the time of their wedding c.1750 (Hull City Council, Wilberforce House Museum).

24 Part of Mogg's *Plan of London* 1810 (Hull City Council, Arts and Humanities Library).

25 John Wesley. Engraving from Cassell's *History of England*, 1905.

26 George Whitfield Preaching. From Cassell's *History of England*, 1905.

27 Entrance to the Dock, by Robert Thew, 1787 (Hull City Council, Ferens Art Gallery).

28 Charlotte Street Hull, from a drawing by F.S.Smith, 1883 (Hull City Council, Wilberforce House Museum).

29 Sir Henry Etherington in hunting regalia. From the painting in the possession of the Hull and East Yorkshire Hospitals NHS Trust.

30 The Grandstand at Beverley Racecourse. From Oliver's *History of Beverley*, 1829.

31 William Wilberforce, an undated sketch (Hull City Council, Wilberforce House Museum).

32 The Town of Hull in 1784, from the plan by Robert Thew (Hull City Council, Local Studies Library).

33 David Hartley. From T.Tindall Wildridge's *Old and New Hull*, 1889.

34 The Hull Poll Book of 1780 (Hull City Council, Local Studies Library).

35 William Pitt the Younger. Engraving from Cassell's *History of England*, 1905.

36 Charles James Fox. Engraving from Cassell's *History of England*, 1905.

37 The Polling, by William Hogarth. From a set of four engravings produced at the time of the parliamentary elections of 1750. From Cassell's *History of England*, 1905.

38 Thomas Thompson. From a copy of a portrait by John Russell (Hull City Council, Maritime Museum).

39 Isaac Milner. Engraving from *The City and the School*, Hull Grammar School, 1979.

40 William Wilberforce at the age of 29, by John Rising (Hull City Council, Wilberforce House Museum).

41 The Triangular Trade (Hull City Council, Wilberforce House Museum).

42 Scene on the West Coast of Africa, by Francois-Auguste Biard (Hull City Council, Wilberforce House Museum).

43 Thomas Clarkson, from a portrait by A.E.Chalons (Hull City Council, Wilberforce House Museum).

44 Group of clergymen at the Wilberforce Oak, Holwood Estate, undated photograph (Hull City Council, Wilberforce House Museum).

45 The Liverpool slave ship "Brooks" (Hull City Council, Wilberforce House Museum).

46 William Pitt addressing the House of Commons on the French declaration of war 1793, by Karl Anton Hickel. By permission of the National Portrait Gallery.

47 William Wilberforce, from an engraving published in Germany in 1795 (Hull City Council, Wilberforce House Museum).

48. "Am I not a man and a brother" (Hull City Council, Wilberforce House Museum).

49 Olaudah Equiano. From the painting at the Royal Albert Museum, by permission of Exeter City Council Museums and Art Galleries.

50 Battersea Rise House, Clapham Common (Hull City Council, Local Studies Library).

51 Barbara Wilberforce aged 24, portrait by John Russell, 1801. By kind permission of the owners.

52 Broomfield Lodge, Clapham Common. From a photograph taken in 1904 (Hull City Council, Wilberforce House Museum).

53 Letter from William Wilberforce to William Hayley dated 22 September 1807 (Hull City Council, Local Studies Library).

54 Letter from Wilberforce to the Freeholders of Yorkshire, 1807 (Hull City Council, Wilberforce House Museum).

55 Wilberforce/Milton handbill from the election of 1807. From T.Tindall Wildridge's *Wilberforce Souvenir*, 1884.

56 Thomas Perronet Thompson (Hull City Council, Wilberforce House Museum).

57 Extracts from the *Hull Advertiser* of December 27 1800 and January 17 1801 (Hull City Council, Local Studies Library).

58 St Peter's Church Drypool. From T.Tindall Wildridge's *Old and New Hull*, 1884.

59 Wilberforce and his family in the library at Battersea Rise. Sketch by Marianne Thornton, about 1824. By permission. Photograph supplied by the Courtauld Institute.

60 Bishop Samuel Wilberforce, an undated photograph (Hull City Council, Wilberforce House Museum).

61 Wax model, based on George Richmond's portrait of Wilberforce in the last year of his life (Hull City Council, Wilberforce House Museum).

62 Medallion produced in 1834 to commemorate the abolition of slavery within British colonies (Hull City Council, Wilberforce House Museum).

63 Plan of Hull in 1842 by Goodwill and Lawson (Hull City Council, Local Studies Library).

64 Monument Bridge, Hull. From Sheahan's *History of Hull*, 1866.

65 Wilberforce Column, view of the head of the statue (Harry Cartridge Collection, Maritime Museum, Hull City Council).

66 Wilberforce Column and Queen's Gardens viewed from Hull College in 1997. Photograph by Bill Marsden 1997 (Hull City Council, Local Studies Library).

67 W.Day Keyworth's statue of Wilberforce in the Hull Town Hall, drawn by F.S.Smith 1885 (Hull City Council, Wilberforce House Museum).

68 Smiths Bank, Whitefriargate, from a photograph published in 1903 in Easton's *History of a Banking House*.

69 Advertisement from *Cook's Directory of Hull* for 1897 (Hull City Council, Local Studies Library).

70 John Brown, 1850-1920 (Hull City Council, Local Studies Library).

71 Queen Victoria Square, 28 July 1933. Photograph courtesy of the Hull Daily Mail.

72 Presentation of the bust of Wilberforce, Freetown City Hall, May 1987. Photograph by Barbara Robinson.

73 Paul Robeson, the distinguished American performer and civil rights activist (Hull City Council, Wilberforce House Museum).

74 Desmond Tutu at the Wilberforce Monument 1 February 1989. Picture by Anthony David Baynes.

75 Archbishop Emeritus Desmond Tutu and the Wilberforce Lecture, Queens Gardens, 1999. Photograph copyright Eddie Rolmanis.

Index

Abolition of the Slave Trade Act 58
Africa 39, 41
African slaves 1, 39, 61, 62
Americas 39
Anti-Slavery Society 65
assemblies 26
Assembly Rooms 25
Babington, Thomas 48, 51
Baltic ports 1
Baltic trade 5, 7, 12
Baskett, Reverend Kingsman 24
Battersea Rise House, Clapham 48, 63
Bettering Society 49
Beverley 3, 6, 7, 26, 54
Beverley Gate 3, 68
Bill for the Abolition of Slavery 65
Bill for the Abolition of the Slave Trade 47
Boswell, James 36, 61
Bristol 39, 43
British and Foreign Bible Society 48
Broadley, Robert 26
Broomfield Lodge, Clapham 51, 52
Brown, Alderman John 74, 75
Buxton, Sir Thomas Fowell 65
Cambridge University 26, 27
Castle Yard at York 36, 56
Charity Hall 3
Church Missionary Society 48
Citadel 3
Clapham community 48 ff.
Clark, John 68
Clarkson, Thomas 40, 41, 43, 47, 59, 65
Cobbett, William 61
Cogan, Alderman William 5
Combination Acts 48, 60
Committee for the Effecting of the Abolition of the Slave Trade 41
Corn Bill 60

Corn Laws 60
Defoe, Daniel 3
Driffield 26
elections 30-32, 36, 54-57
emancipation 64, 65
Equiano, Olaudah 47
Evangelicalism 23, 41, 54, 64
Fox, Charles James 33, 46, 47
freemen, (freeholders) 30, 36, 55, 57, 58
Freetown 76, 78
French Republic 46
French Revolution 46, 61
Game Laws 59
Garrison 3, 4
George III 1, 33
Georgian Houses 10, 11
Grammar School, Hull 13, 14, 23, 25
'great change', the 37
Habeas Corpus 60
Hartley, David 31, 40
Haven, the 1, 3
High Street, Hull 3, 7, 9, 11, 12, 15, 36, 54, 64, 74
Highwood Hill 64
Hollar, Wenceslaus 2, 3
Holy Trinity church, Hull 12, 13, 14, 16, 54
Hull Corporation 5, 13, 26, 54, 60, 62, 74
Humber, the 1
Keyworth, W. Day 72, 73
King Billy statue, Hull 14, 16
Kingston Communications 75
Lauriston House, Wimbledon 35
Liverpool 1, 39, 43
Louis XVI of France 46
Macaulay, Zachary 48, 52, 57
Maister family 5. 11
merchants of Hull 1, 5, 7 13, 23, 25
Methodism 22, 37

91

Methodists 22, 23
'middle passage', the 39, 58
Middleton, Sir Charles 40, 41
Milner, Joseph 14, 23, 54
Milner, Isaac 14, 36, 37, 48
Monument Bridge 68, 69
More, Hannah 47, 48, 49, 51
Napoleon 47, 59
Newton, John 37, 41
North Ferriby 9, 13, 26
North Sea trade 1, 5
Old Harbour, Hull 1
Old Palace Yard, London 21, 41, 57
opium 43
Peterloo Massacre 60
Pitt, William 30, 33, 36, 41, 43, 45, 46, 47
Pocklington 6
Pocklington Grammar School 18, 23
Poll Book 32
Port of Hull 1
Practical View of the Prevailing Religious system of Professed Christians in the Higher and Middle Classes in this country, contrasted with Real Christianity 49
Proclamation Society 49
Quakers 40
Queen's Dock 3, 24, 29, 71
Queen's Gardens 68, 71
River Hull 1, 4, 11
Robeson, Paul 79
RSPCA 59
'Saints', the 48
Scarborough 26, 37
Sharp, Granville 40, 41, 48
Sheppard, Thomas 75
Sierra Leone 49, 52, 57, 76-78
slave ship 43, 44
slave trade 39, 41, 43, 46-48, 59
slavery 43, 64, 65
Smith, Abel 19, 26, 35
Smith family of Nottingham 19
Society for the Prevention of Cruelty to Animals 59
Society for the Suppression of Vice 49
St Mary's Church, Beverley 18, 19
St Mary's Church, Lowgate, Hull 7, 9, 14
Sykes, Marianne 35, 51

Sykes family 5, 13, 25, 35, 58, 64
Tarran, Robert Greenwood 71
Thompson, Thomas 35, 54, 57
Thompson, Thomas Perronet 57
Thornton, Henry 48, 49, 51
Thornton, John (Hull merchant) 7, 48
Thornton, Marianne 51, 52
Thornton family 5, 13, 19
trade unions 60
'triangular trade' 39
Tutu, Archbishop Desmond 80, 81
Venn, John 48
Wedgwood, Josiah 47
Wesley, John 3, 22, 23, 40
West Indies 1, 39, 41, 48
Whitfield, George 22, 23
Wilberforce, Mrs Barbara, nee Spooner (W.W.'s wife) 50, 51, 52, 54, 62
Wilberforce, Mrs Elizabeth (W.W.'s mother) 7, 9, 19, 26, 35, 54
Wilberforce, Mrs Hannah, nee Thornton (W.W.'s aunt) 19, 20, 23, 24
Wilberforce, Henry 52, 53, 62
Wilberforce, Robert (W.W.'s father) 7, 9, 12, 17, 19
Wilberforce, Robert Isaac 52, 62, 65
Wilberforce, Samuel 52, 62, 64, 65
Wilberforce, Sarah (W.W.'s sister, known as Sally) 9, 35, 54
Wilberforce, William (W.W.'s son) 52, 64
Wilberforce, William (W.W.'s uncle) 7, 19, 20, 23, 24, 27
Wilberforce, Alderman William (W.W.'s grandfather) 5, 9, 13, 19, 23, 27
Wilberforce Column 68 ff.
Wilberforce House 9-11, 73 ff.
Wilberforce House Museum 73 ff.
Wilberforce Lecture 77, 80
Wilberforce Medallion 80
Wilberforce Monument 68 ff.
Wilberforce Oak 42
Wilberforce Statue 73
Wilberfoss 6, 7, 23
Wilkinson, Tate 25
Wimbledon 19, 24, 35
workhouse 3
working class 61